Getting Darwin Wrong

Getting Darwin Wrong

Why Evolutionary Psychology
Won't Work

Brendan Wallace

imprint-academic.com

Published in the UK by
Imprint Academic, PO Box 200, Exeter EX5 5YX, UK

Published in the USA by Imprint Academic,
Philosophy Documentation Center
PO Box 7147, Charlottesville, VA 22906-7147, USA

ISBN 9781845402075

A CIP catalogue record for this book is available from the
British Library and US Library of Congress

Contents

Introduction

To begin with, I should state what this book is NOT about. It is not (at least, not directly) about the so-called 'nature-nurture' debate. Nor is it about whether or not Darwinian theories of evolution can or should be used to help understand the human mind (in my opinion they should). Nor is it about other recent attempts (most notoriously the study of 'sociobiology' which was popular in the 1970s) to apply Darwin's theories to human psychology.

Instead it is a discussion of a highly specific branch of psychology, which, using the standard term, I will call Evolutionary Psychology (EP). I should stress here that I am using the capitalised form to discuss EP *as it actually exists.* It may well be the case (and, in fact, probably *is* the case) that there are other ways (i.e. other than EP) to apply Darwin's theories to the so-called human sciences, and it also may well be the case that these other approaches are not vulnerable to the criticisms that will be detailed in this book. But I'm going to be discussing reality here, what *is* the case as opposed to what might have been the case, and so the whole subject of this text will be, to repeat, EP as it actually exists at present: i.e. EP as it is explicated in the various books written by Steven Pinker, Leda Cosmides, John Tooby, and others who would (I think) identify themselves as Evolutionary Psychologists.

Whereas the nature-nurture debate goes back to Plato, and the attempt to apply Darwinian theories to human psychology goes back to … well, Darwin, EP is an extremely modern science. Although its roots, as I hope to show, go back to the 1950s and 1960s, the movement announced itself to the world with the publication, in 1992, of *The Adapted Mind: Evolutionary Psychology and the Generation of Culture* (edited by Jerome Barkow, Leda Cosmides and John Tooby).[1] This book was in two sections, the second section of which consisted mainly of empirical work. However it is the first section which concerns us here, as it was, perhaps, the first coherent attempt to lay out a general theoretical framework for EP. Here the most important essay is 'The Psychological Foundations of Culture' (jointly written by Cosmides and Tooby), which has some claim to be the founding document of EP.

The Adapted Mind was, by academic standards, a smash hit. In Google Scholar at the time of writing, it is stated to have been referred to in 1001 other academic texts: a huge number for a book of academic essays. However, academic texts generally speaking don't set the world on fire, and it was the young American psychologist Steven Pinker who was the St Paul of the new movement: travelling throughout the world, spreading (and popularising) the new psychological Gospel. Pinker had a lot of things going for him: not least the fact that he was young (for an academic), good looking (for an academic …), and was capable of providing media friendly soundbites on late night TV and radio discussion programmes. He also proved expert at something that academics frequently stumble over: writing detailed but clear expositions of complex ideas in a way that lends itself to being serialised in newspapers. He had also previously written a top-selling 'pop-sci' book *The Language Instinct* in 1994.

And so, when Pinker wrote *How the Mind Works* (published 1997) he was in the ideal position to become a scientific

---

1 Cosmides and Tooby had written articles for journals on these themes before, but it was *The Adapted Mind* that first set out EP as a new movement in psychology.

celebrity. And in the eyes of the general public, *How the Mind Works* became THE book of EP. As Pinker was the first to admit it was not a particularly original book, drawing heavily on the work of Cosmides and Tooby, as well as earlier work in cognitive science, but its flowing prose style, combined with the numerous articles and interviews Pinker did to promote it, almost guaranteed it would become a bestseller. And it did. The book won the Los Angeles Times Science Book Prize, was shortlisted for the Pullitzer and topped bestseller lists the world over. Pinker followed this up with *The Blank Slate: The Modern Denial of Human Nature* (2002) which drew political and social morals from EP. Again, this was a bestseller.

Of course, *How the Mind Works* also provoked a storm of controversy, which is never a bad thing from a publisher's point of view (as Andy Warhol once remarked: when you get your reviews in, don't read them, weigh them). For example, in 2000, Hilary and Steven Rose published a book of essays entitled *Alas, Poor Darwin: Arguments against Evolutionary Psychology* which attempted to rebut the basic claims of EP. Richard Lewontin, Stephen Jay Gould, and David J. Buller are amongst the others who have written books attacking EP, with Pinker, Cosmides, Tooby and others writing rebuttals of the rebuttals, and at the time of writing the whole controversy seems likely to rumble on for decades.

So: why another book discussing EP? To begin with, it might well be thought wise to write a book after the initial storm has died down. Far too much of the initial discussion created much heat but threw little light on the basic claims of EP, but led instead to a situation where various terms of abuse ('relativist', 'determinist', 'reductionist') were thrown about, without much thought being given to defining these terms, or deciding whether or not EP (or its opponents) were guilty of the myriad intellectual 'sins' of which they were accused. Moreover, there was a (to my mind) reprehensible tendency to infer political tendencies from the various scientific theories proposed. EP has political connotations of course: all scientific theories (including those of theoretical physics) have political implications. But it's grossly unfair to argue that just because a theory might lead to 'right wing' (or 'left wing') conclusions that therefore it must be rejected. As an old philosophy lecturer once told us as fresh eyed undergraduates in our first years of University: if something has been *proven* to be true, *you just have to accept it,* whether you like its implications or not. 'It makes me feel bad, therefore it's false' is not an argument.

But there's another issue as well, and that has to do with the relation of EP to psychology itself.

I don't think it's greatly controversial to state that mainstream academic psychology in the 1980s was based on two main 'philosophies' of psychology. They were not precisely the same, but the clearly had much in common. These views were the *information processing* model of cognition, and the theory of *cognitivism*. These two theories in turn were clearly related to a third theory, more fashionable in AI and computing than in psychology, but still highly influential, the theory of *computationalism*.

Since these terms, vastly influential though they have been in academia, are unlikely to ring too many bells outside of it, some explanation is in order. To begin with I should state that the 'borders' of these theories are 'fuzzy'. There is no 'set book' which defines cognitivism in the same way that *The Adapted Mind* defines EP, and some people's definitions of the word would be different from mine. Nevertheless, I think my own definitions aren't too far from the truth, and, whilst they may not be 'objective' I think I can demonstrate that at least some other psychologists agree with them, to a greater or lesser extent.

To take them in order then. The **information processing** view of human cognition is, as the name suggests, the idea that human cognition consists mainly (or exclusively) of the *processing of information*. Now there's a sense in which this claim is trivially and obviously true, but (and this distinction is sometimes blurred, even by psychologists who should know better) the academic definition of this phrase goes much further than the 'lay' definition. In academia, information has (or should have) a highly specific definition. Information was defined (for science, in this context) by Claude Shannon in his paper 'A Mathematical Theory of Communication' (1948). This paper was essentially the foundation stone for modern information science, and it gave a precise and *mathematical* definition of the word 'information'. Moreover, Shannon also helped to provide a coherent theory of what it was to *process* information (what this was will be discussed later), and, therefore, a definition of what an 'information processor' might be.

The 'information processing' view of psychology is simply the view that the brain actually is (or is 'to all intents and purposes') an information processor (i.e. in the same way as a digital computer is an information processer).

The second of the 'triad' of theories that were widely held by psychologists in the 1960s and 1970s is **cognitivism**. Cognitivism is the belief that cognition is the manipulation of *symbols* by *rules* or algorithms. Why psychologists believe that this might be the case is rather a long story, which will be developed in later chapters, but the key point here is that this 'action' of the rules on the symbols is supposed to happen in, so to speak, 'internal' cognitive space (which is not exactly the same as the brain space between your ears, although these symbols and rules should, in theory, always be reducable to brain states).

Finally we have **computationalism**, the belief that the human brain is (or can me usefully compared to) a digital computer.

Now psychologists reading this will already be ready to take issue with me, as the definitions above are by no means uncontroversial. And there are other subdivisions that philosophers will be familiar with (for example the debate between 'functionalists' and 'representationalists') which we don't need to into here.

Nonetheless, I think most psychologists would accept that a great deal (or possibly all) of what came to be known as the 'cognitive revolution' can be described under one or all of the three categories above. And it is *unquestionably* true that from the late 'sixties until roughly the mid 'eighties, psychologists became far less interested in elaborations of 'stimulus-response' theory, and experiments on animals (i.e. behaviourism) and instead became interested in experiments involving humans which at least alluded to the idea that the brain was a form of information processor, possibly similar to a digital computer. For the purposes of simplicity, I will simply use 'cognitivism' as the general word to describe the shared assumptions, not just of cognitivism 'proper' but also of the 'information processing' view of cognition and 'computationalism'.

So the argument of this book is (I think) novel and quite simple. It is this. Evolutionary Psychology is NOT (as it is normally taken to be) an unproblematic adaption of Darwinian theory to the science of psychology. Instead, EP is an adaption of a specific 'school' of psychology: that of 'cognitivism' (or the 'information processing view of human cognition' or 'computationalism'). Essentially EP is *an attempt to reinterpret and restate the basic precepts of cognitivism within a Darwinian framework.*

This seems like a controversial argument but actually, a careful reading of the seminal works of Cosmides, Tooby, Pinker, and other associated with EP shows that they have always been fairly clear about what EP really is, and what they are trying to do. I will also attempt to show that Cosmides *et al.* were forced to adopt their cognitivist position because of certain assumptions they began with about what psychology is and should be, and that these assumptions themselves are by no means unproblematic.

The next stage in my argument (which will apparently take us a long way away from a discussion of Darwinism but which in fact does not) will be a discussion of 'cognitivism'. Is cognitivism true? If the first part of my argument holds, then if cognitivism is 'wrong' (i.e. inaccurate, a scientific theory that does not make adequate predictions or which is otherwise flawed in some way) then EP *could not be true, and its relationship to Darwinism is irrelevant.* The corollary of this is, of course that, if cognitivism is, essentially the correct way of looking at human psychology than EP, or something similar to it, *must* be true. That is, assuming that Darwinism/

natural selection is the only way of explaining the evolution of Man (and that thesis will be assumed, not argued in this text) then cognitivism must adapt itself to Darwinism, not vice versa: therefore, a cognitivist Darwinism (i.e. some form or adaption of EP) really is the only way to go to create a genuinely scientific psychology.

Finally I'll go on to discuss the way in which the main EP writers have, so to speak, extrapolated obscure debates in the history of psychology and expanded them until they have become whole philosophies of life: hence Steve Pinker's steady progress from a linguist (*The Language Instinct*) to a cognitive/evolutionary psychologist (*How the Mind Works*) to a moral/political philosopher (*The Blank Slate*).

It should be noted that EP is still an expanding science, and that there is now (for example) a school of developmental evolutionary psychology, evolutionary psychological neuro-science, and so forth. It might seem churlish for me not to discuss these secondary developments. But in actual fact, for the purposes of this argument, they are irrelevant. Either cognitivism is true or it's not, and either the adaption of EP by Cosmides, Tooby, Pinker *et al.* are true or they are not, and further adaptions and developments (which overwhelmingly assume the truth of the Cosmides/Tooby/Pinker approach) are really irrelevant.

However, to begin at the beginning.

Chapter One

In the beginning, there was sociobiology. Or at least, so it has been claimed.

The word 'sociobiology' first came to the attention of the public with the publication of *Sociobiology: The New Synthesis* in 1975 (Wilson, 2000). This book was written by Edward O. Wilson, an entomologist who had built his academic reputation on his studies of ant behaviour. *Sociobiology* was highly influenced by W.D. Hamilton, a biologist, and Robert Trivers, another biologist (by which I mean they were trained, academically, as biologists).

Given the amount of controversy this book caused with its description of human psychology, new readers of *Sociobiology: the New Synthesis* are often surprised to find out that this is *primarily* a work of biology, not psychology. Indeed, it was voted by the Animal Behaviour Society the most important book on *animal* behaviour of all time (Wilson, 2006). And, apart from the last chapter, this is what it is about: animal behaviour. It is only in the last, tentative and speculative chapter, that Wilson attempted to apply the lessons of biology and natural selection to humans.

As stated in the introduction, the book you are now reading is not about sociobiology. However we have to discuss it here because sociobiology is generally agreed to have been a failure. The reason for this is simple. Sociobiology was a theory about the present. It asked: what are the causes of *contemporary* human behaviours, and in what way do they maximise evolutionary 'fitness'? For example, a sociobiologist might say that I own a car because an expensive car would help me find a mate, or something of that sort. The problem with this of course, is that this starts to sound very similar to the sort of 'explanations' found in Freudian psychoanalysis, in which cars, cigars and pens are 'obviously' phallic symbols. Counter-explanations are easily explained away. Sociobiology in other words, explains too much, and provides too 'deep' an explanation for things that surely have simpler (more 'proximal') causes (Malik, 2001). And that is why *opponents* of Evolutionary Psychology (EP) tend to allege that EP is merely sociobiology updated. *Proponents* of EP on the other hand, are usually very keen to make the point that EP is a completely new science with no links to the earlier sociobiology.

Part of the argument of this book is that the proponents of EP are right. Contemporary EP does *not* derive or at least does not derive *directly*, from sociobiology. To see why, look at the academic backgrounds of the people who created sociobiology. To repeat, these scholars tended to be biologists, who had academic training in biology, and who taught in University biology departments.

To see the differences between sociobiology and EP, let's now look at the backgrounds of the pre-eminent thinkers in EP.

Now, in the development of EP, overwhelmingly the most important writers are Leda Cosmides and John Tooby. It is them who popularised the phrase, who wrote the most commonly cited papers in the field, and who wrote the founding text of the new science *The Adapted Mind: Evolutionary Psychology and the Generation of Culture* (Barkow, Cosmides and Tooby, 1992).

Now, Leda Cosmides, it's true, originally studied biology. However, her post-graduate degree (PhD) was in cognitive science. And the academic work she completed after that (post-doctoral) was under the guidance of Roger Shepard, another cognitive scientist (indeed, his magnum opus is entitled *Toward a Universal Law of Generalization for Psychological Science*, which is an illuminating title, as we will see) (UC Santa Barbara Webpage, 2002).

John Tooby, on the other hand, was trained as an anthropologist. He is currently a professor of anthropology at the University of California (UCSB webpage: 2004).

Jerome H. Barkow, the third editor of *The Adapted Mind* is another anthropologist, whose undergraduate degree was in psychology (Dalhousie University Webpage 2002). David M. Buss, another proponent of EP, is currently Professor of Psychology at the University of Texas at Austin (University of Texas at Austin, 2009). Donald Symons, who wrote the other key 'position paper' in *The Adapted Mind*, is another anthropologist. Steven Pinker, despite the fact that his early work was in linguistics (another significant fact) has a BA and a PhD in cognitive science and currently works in the Psychology Department at Harvard (Harvard University, 2003).

We can infer from this information the initial argument of this book. Sociobiology (which, beyond the works of Hamilton, Trivers and Wilson has its roots in the Darwinian synthesis of Fisher and Mayr: the so-called 'Modern Synthesis'), was *primarily* a theory of **animal behaviour**, created by *biologists*. EP, on the other hand, is *primarily* a theory of **human cognition**, created by *cognitive scientists and anthropologists*, the vast majority of whom, it should be noted, have little or no biological training.

There's another point that has to be made here and it concerns not just the first wave of Evolutionary Psychologist's academic backgrounds, but when they were trained. Cosmides received her PhD in cog-sci in 1985. Tooby received his PhD in 1989. Barkow received his PhD in 1970. Pinker received his PhD in 1979. So, the 'guiding lights' of EP received their basic academic training roughly between the early 1970s and the mid to late 1980s. In other words they all graduated from American universities in the 1970s and 1980s.

These important facts have been overlooked by most critics of EP, because critics of EP, generally speaking, consider it to be a theory of biology which has been applied (wrongly, it is often stated) to psychology. But, I will argue, this gets things the wrong way round. As the backgrounds of the main EP scholars shows, EP is *essentially* a theory of psychology and anthropology (and linguistics) with some biology added, as it were, on top. And it was a theory that arose in a very specific time and place: in the United States between the early 'seventies and the mid to late' eighties.

Sociobiology is false, or at least a gross over-simplification (as a theory of human behaviour: it has been productive when applied to animals). It failed because, in explaining everything, it explained nothing: evolutionary explanations it seems, are the wrong kind of explanations for our everyday behaviours. Why, therefore is Evolutionary Psychology different? The first difference is the one that gets all the attention, but is, I will argue, relatively trivial. EP argues that, yes, it's facile to explain contemporary behaviour in terms of evolution. But, thinkers in the EP tradition continue, it's *not* facile to look at evolution in the context of the environment for which we actually evolved. We evolved (according to the thinkers of EP) 'for' the stone age Savannah in Africa tens of thousands of years ago, and spent the vast majority of 'our' lifetime as a species in that environment. Therefore that is, so to speak, our cognitively 'natural' environment. We have adapted (evolutionarily speaking) for *that* environment and not for our current environment. So what EP does is look at the extent to which evolution shaped us for the environment of prehistoric Africa.

OK fair enough, one might argue. But so what? Why can't we have continued to evolve, or shown behavioural/cognitive plasticity? Why should we be forever 'stuck' in the Savannahs of Africa, cognitively speaking? Here is where EP radically differs from sociobiology. Because, unlike sociobiology, the thinkers of EP claim to have an answer to that question, and also an answer to the question of what 'causes' behaviour generally. Whereas sociobiology dealt with 'distal' causation (what ultimately causes something) which was evolution, the mechanisms of proximal causation were left vague. But EP is different. It explains human behaviour in terms of distal explanation by evolution, but also explains human behaviour in proximal terms.

But before we meet this proximal mechanism which, according to EP, causes our actions, we have to understand the intellectual context of the origins of EP, an intellectual context that, as we shall see, the main thinkers of EP essentially took for granted. As we have seen, these scholars were mainly psychologists and anthropologists. So we have to ask: what was going on in cognitive science/ anthropology and linguistics in this time period in the United States? What was being taught? What was 'in'? And this is not an uninteresting question because the period between, roughly 1970 and 1985 was the highpoint in the United States[1] of what I have called in the Introduction 'Cognitivism'. Other names for cognitivism might be 'computationalism' or the 'information processing view of cognition'.

The idea that cognition 'just is' the processing of information, that thoughts relate to the brain in the same way that computer programs relate to the computer, and that, in some non-trivial sense, the brain is like a digital computer (albeit in an abstract use of that phrase), were widely accepted in American psychology departments when the dominant figures in EP received their basic academic training. And, as we shall see, with a few exceptions, the main thinkers of EP took these assumptions for granted, and used them as the basis for their efforts to Darwinise the social sciences.

To see where the guiding lights of EP are 'coming from' therefore, we should look at what cognitivism is, how it arose, and why it was so popular in the 1970s and 1980s. And this involves looking at what preceded cognitivism. Because it's only by looking at what it superseded that we can see what cognitivism was really all about.

---

1 Other countries, especially European countries, were considerably more sceptical.

Psychology in the 'West'

'Modern' experimental psychology (which is what we will be talking about here: in other words, I will not be discussing psycho-analysis and the various non-experimental psychologies that ultimately can trace their origins to Freud) began with Wilhelm Wundt, who set up the first psychology laboratory at the University of Leipzig in 1879. He also described psychology's first method ('introspectionism') and its first 'philosophy' ('structuralism'). Introspectionism, as its name suggests, was a methodology of getting subjects to report their own 'internal' cognitive processes. The verbal description of these internal cognitive states would reveal the cognitive 'structures' that were it was alleged, common to all humans (Kukla and Walmsley, 2006).

The problem with Wundt's theories and practices is inherent in the use of the word 'introspectionism'. The key problem for the new science was reproducibility. On performing tasks, different subjects would put forward different 'reasons' for their behaviours, and it was difficult (or impossible) to create generalised theories of cognition based on this data. What is interesting about introspectionism is that it was an explicitly Cartesian theory (a word that will be explained fully later on: suffice to say at the moment that introspectionism followed in an intellectual tradition begun by the 17th century French philosopher Descartes), and that, as Kukla and Walmsley put it: '*All* major 20th century theories of psychology were reactions to introspective psychology' (Kukla and Walmsley, 2006: 23) (emphasis added).

However, as a result of the reproducibility problem, a new school of *behaviourism* arose to challenge structuralism in the 1920s and 1930s. I might add that if that last clause were to be read out publicly in a psychology lecture, perhaps the lights should dim, and a recording of thunder in the distance should be played. Certainly no word, nowadays, strikes more fear into the hearts of most contemporary psychologists than 'behaviourism'. As the joke has it, most psychology departmental heads would rather see a burglar in their office than a behaviourist. Even now, many anti-cognitivist arguments can be seemingly stopped in their tracks by someone simply stating: 'but that's just behaviourism!'.

But behaviourism is particularly interesting for our current discussion because cognitivism arose as a direct result of (and reaction to) behaviourism and the behaviourism-cognitivism 'battle' in the 1950s and 1960s is the 'background' for the first wave of Evolutionary Psychology.

Behaviourism

It might seem strange that the battle between the cognitivists and the behaviourists was fought with such ferocity, as they shared a common aim: to put psychology on a genuinely scientific footing. Of course, this implied a shared and 'objective' definition of just precisely what 'science' actually was/is was available: which is, of course, not necessarily the case. Nevertheless it was the subjectivity of the structuralists that the behaviourists objected to: when asked for details of their cognitive 'inner states', even when manifesting the same behaviour, some subjects produced one reason, some another. Making an assumption (and this *is* an assumption) that true science is and should be about creating a model of the regularities of human behaviour (that is, to infer scientific ['objective'] laws of human behaviour) the behaviourists 'cut the Gordian knot' by simply stating that the realm of the 'inner', whatever that meant, was simply no longer to be part of genuine psychology. From now on, psychology would be about the 'outer' only: that is, it would be about behaviour. And not just any form of behaviour either, but behaviour that could be controlled: i.e. behaviour that was a *response* to a specific *stimulus*. And of course, the experiments that would demonstrated these lawful reactions to 'stimuli' were easier to carry out on rats and other 'lower' animals than humans. Hence the behaviourists' emphasis on experiments on animals (including, most notoriously, rats).

The first point to be made about behaviourism is that there is absolutely nothing ridiculous or 'reactionary' about its plan to put experimental psychology on a firm scientific basis. Indeed, their arguments against 'structuralism' had some force: the structuralists gathered much data, but what any of it actually *meant* was questionable. One might ultimately disapprove of the behaviourist's disavowal of the 'inner' but it was a serious argument, which deserved serious arguments in reply. The second point is that, despite much sneering over the idea of 'rat psychology', it is entirely justifiable (assuming one accepts the basis tenets of natural selection) to carry out experiments on 'lower' animals in an attempt to see to what extent the behaviours exhibited are recapitulated in 'higher' animals (i.e. us). Indeed, one might argue that it is more justifiable in terms of a genuine evolutionary psychology than the structuralist and cognitivist obsession with *human* cognition (and *only* with human cognition).

But there's a more important issue here and it's with the behaviourist's basic view of human nature. As James B. Watson (who essentially started the movement) once stated:

> Give me a dozen healthy infants, well-formed, and my own specified world to bring them up in and I'll guarantee to take any one at random and train him to become any type of specialist ... doctor, lawyer, artist, merchant-chief and, yes even beggar-man and thief, regardless of his talents, abilities, vocations, and race of his ancestors. I am going beyond my facts and I admit it, but *so have the advocates of the contrary and they have been doing it for many thousands of years'*. (Watson, 1997: 82) (emphasis added: the last sentence of that paragraph is rarely quoted by those who oppose behaviourism).

The essence of behaviourism, we are always told, is a denial of (or at least, lack of interest in) cognitive 'inner states', and this is true. However as the quote above demonstrates, and even a brief read through the works of Watson and Skinner demonstrates, behaviourism is better seen as a self-conscious attempt to re-orientate psychology to be the study of *learned behaviour.*[2] And it's pretty obvious why this had to be the case. If you don't accept the existence of 'internal' static, cognitive 'modules' or 'structures' then obviously the brain becomes a much more 'fluid' and 'plastic' affair than might otherwise be thought to be the case. So *learning* becomes the key feature of human behaviour that behaviourism set out to explain.

Behaviourism in Context

This book is not about the history of psychology and we aren't going to go over in great detail the ins and outs of debates about the future of psychology that took place in the mid-twentieth century. But what should be stressed here is that despite their interest in 'lower' animals (and make no mistake, the behaviourists were just as keen on Darwinism as the most aggressive proponent of EP today), the behaviourists were not 'reductionists' *per se*, as they were uninterested in 'reducing' behaviour to the cognitive 'components' that might lie behind it. Indeed, because of their philosophical assumptions, they could hardly begin to do this, even if they wanted to (disbelief in 'cognitive components' or, for that matter, cognitive anything, was of course the defining feature of behaviourism). Behaviourists were interested in brain-body *behaviour, viewed as a whole.*

There are many myths about behaviourism, and perhaps the most hard to shift is that behaviourism was the only important school of psychology between (say) 1920 and 1965. In actuality it always had competitors: psycho-analysis, obviously, but also, within experimental psychology, the German 'Gestalt' group, the 'ecological' school of J.J. Gibson, the Activity Theory of Vygotsky, and the developmental school of Jean Piaget all challenged its hegemony. Nevertheless, it was a hugely influential movement (especially in the United States) and it's probably fair to say that behaviourist academics had

---

2 In other words, just to be even more specific, behaviourism is a kind of learning theory: i.e. a theory about learning.

a lot of power in the (American and British) academy by the 1950s.

This is the background for the emergence of 'cognitivism' which first arose in the late 1950s and which had become the dominant school of psychology in the Anglo-American world by the early 1980s. It's important to point out to readers who are not familiar with academia that the academic world is not as different from the 'real' world of business as it sometimes makes out. In both worlds people struggle for jobs and promotions and these struggles are essentially about money and power. And so when cognitivism arose in the late '50s, there was a fundamental problem: most of the 'senior' posts in academia were held by behaviourists.

What followed, therefore, was a power struggle, with the 'younger generation' of cognitivists attempting to gain those precious academic posts from the 'older generation'. And the best way to do this was to discredit them (or at least their beliefs).

This accounts for the extraordinarily aggressive tone of the younger cognitivists. Indeed, this battle for intellectual hegemony was so violent (rhetorically speaking) that, as we shall see, many of the cognitivists have simply never got past it and have spent their careers continually watching the 'frontiers' of cognitivism, nervously looking for hypothetical invading hordes of behaviourists on the outside, and quisling backsliders from the true gospel of cognitivism on the inside.

But this avoids the basic question that needs to be asked here, which is, precisely, what was cognitivism, why did it arise, and why did people find it so convincing a theory of human cognition?

The Rise of Cognitivism

Cognitivism is such an amorphous term that in many ways it means all things to all people. Indeed, within psychology it can be (and has been) applied to almost everyone who is not an out and out behaviourist.

However, this book is about Evolutionary Psychology, so the best way to look at cognitivism in this context, I think, is to let the Evolutionary Psychologists themselves state what cognitivism means to them. Here no one is more eloquent or clearer than Steven Pinker, in *How the Mind Works*. Remember: this is Pinker describing the **core, basic** tenets of EP.

> The Mind is not the brain but what the brain does ... the brain's special status comes from a special thing the brain does ... that special thing is information processing, or computation. Information and computation reside in patterns of data and in relations of logic that are independent of the physical medium that carries them. This insight, first expressed by the mathematician Alan Turing, the computer scientists Alan Newell, Herbert Simon and Marvin Minsky, and the philosophers Hilary Putnam and Jerry Fodor is now called the computational theory of mind. It is one of the great ideas of intellectual history, for it solves one of the puzzles that make up the 'mind-body problem': how to connect the ethereal world of meaning and intention, the stuff with our mental lives, with a physical hunk of matter like the brain ... the computational theory of mind resolves the paradox. It says that beliefs and desires are *information,* incarnated as configurations of symbols ... the computational theory of mind is indispensable in addressing the questions we long to answer ... without the computational theory it is impossible to make sense of the evolution of the mind. (Pinker, 2003: 24–27).

I make no apology for this long quote, as *this* (and not Darwinian natural selection) is the core idea of EP. It is the bedrock of EP. It is the foundation stone on which EP rests, and if it is not true, then EP is not (*could not be*) true. Pinker goes on to argue (and here we really get to the nub of the matter):

> The mind, I claim, is not a single organ but a system of organs, which we can think of as ... mental modules. The entities now commonly evoked to explain the mind – such as *general intelligence*, a capacity to create culture, and *multipurpose*

learning strategies – will surely go the way of protoplasm in biology and of earth, air, fire and water in physics.' (Pinker, 2003: 31) (emphasis added).

Here, again, we see the extent to which Pinker's core position has been misunderstood because so many of the scholars who have attacked EP are not psychologists and simply do not see where Pinker is coming from. But the phrases 'multipurpose learning strategies' and 'general intelligence' give the game away. What Pinker is doing here (as an orthodox 1980s mainstream cognitivist) is *attacking behaviourism*. Because it is, of course, (as we have seen) the emphasis on learning that sets behaviourism apart from cognitivism. To repeat: behaviourism's view of the mind was 'general' and 'holistic' (hence the reference to general intelligence) whereas cognitivists tend to see the mind in terms of discrete mental modules. And it was the behaviourists who tended to emphasise the importance of 'multi-purpose learning strategies', as opposed to cognitivists who explained behaviour in terms of pre-'installed' mental apparatus, which functioned like pre-installed computer programs.

But, to recap: Pinker gives us a clue here to his view of cognitivism: he claims it was set out by Alan Turing, Newell, Simon and Minsky, and Putnam and Fodor. Who were these men? What did they say? The answer to these questions will give us insights into what Pinker means by the 'computational theory of mind'.

The Cognitivist Vanguard

The first surprise might be to discover that none of the originators of cognitivism were actually psychologists (and of course, none of them were biologists either). Instead they were mathematicians (Turing) management theorists (Newell) political scientists (Simon), workers in 'Artificial Intelligence'

(Minsky), or philosophers (Putnam, Fodor). The other great precursor of cognitivism, Noam Chomsky, is a linguist.[3]

However, in a sense to concentrate on their different academic 'upbringings' is misleading, because in actuality all these scholars had one major interest in common: the computer and/or mathematical modelling of human 'cognition' (or to be specific, what they took to be the *essence* of cognition). This becomes clearer if we look at the thinking of the 'earliest' of these thinkers: Turing.

Turing

Alan Turing (born 1912) was a British mathematician who is generally considered to be one of the fathers of computer science. Turing is best known, nowadays, for his description of a Turing Machine, which he first sketched out in his classic, if terrifying sounding, paper: 'On Computable Numbers, with an Application to the *Entscheidungsproblem*'. (Turing, 1937). The key point to remember about a Turing Machine is that it is an abstract description of a possible computer device, a determinist, algorithm 'driven' machine to solve logical problems.

What has Turing's thesis as expressed in this paper got to do with psychology? To quote John Searle: 'Turing's thesis says that there is a Universal Turing Machine which can simulate any Turing Machine'. Now if we put these two together we have the result that a Universal Turing Machine can implement any algorithm whatever.

But now, what made this result so exciting? What made it send shivers up and down the spines of a whole generation of young workers in artificial intelligence is the following thought: *Suppose the brain is a Universal Turing Machine.'* (Goldman, 1993: 836–837). Why did Turing think this? To quote Searle again:

---

3 I argue later on that Claude Shannon also helped create cognitivism: Shannon was an engineer who worked in telephony.

It is clear that at least some human mental abilities are algorithmic. For example, I can consciously do long division by going through the steps of an algorithm for solving long division problems. It is furthermore a consequence of the Church-Turing thesis and Turing's theorem that *anything a human can do algorithmically can be done on a Universal Turing Machine.* I can implement, for example, the very same algorithm that I use for long division on a digital computer. In such a case, as described by Turing (1950), both I, the human computer, and the mechanical computer are implementing the same algorithm, I am doing it consciously, the mechanical computer non-consciously. Now it seems reasonable to suppose there might also be a whole lot of mental processes going on in my brain non-consciously which are also computational. And if so, we could find out how the brain works by simulating these very processes on a digital computer. Just as we got a computer simulation of the processes for doing long division, so we could get a computer simulation of the processs for understanding language, visual perception, categorization, etc. (Searle, 1990) (italics added).

I have emphasised the sections of this paragraph that I think are particularly important, because this, to me, really states the essence of cognitivism: the idea that at least some, perhaps most, perhaps all, elements of human cognition are algorithmic in nature.

Before we go on, it's probably best to have a definition of the word 'algorithm' in order to make crystal clear what's being implied here.

To quote the dictionary an algorithm is: 'A step-by-step problem-solving procedure, especially an established, recursive *computational procedure* for solving a problem in a finite number of steps.' (*American Heritage Dictionary*, 2009) (italics added).

It's important to state this because as the brushing past of the issue ('It is clear …') demonstrates, many computer sciences take the 'cognition=algorithms' equation as being axiomatic. But it's actually a pretty strong claim, and one that (*pace* Pinker) many people do not accept: because if one 'unpacks' it' this is really the claim that much (perhaps most, perhaps all) human cognition is really computational in nature. After all, what 'powers' the computer programs which we all use on a day to day basis, and via which I am now writing this sentence (on a desktop PC)? Computer programs are really long strings of algorithms: deterministic step by instructions to tell the computer to do stuff. And Turing took it for granted that at least some cognition is done in the same way. Note that if one reads Turing's original papers he does not claim that cognition is 'like' computation. He claims that it *is* computation, in an abstract sense (i.e. cognition is 'powered', so to speak, by algorithms) (Turing, 1950).

It's this idea, that cognition equals the deterministic 'unrolling' of algorithms that was crucial, because another 'thing' that quite definitely uses algorithms is the digital computer. And this link permits another question to be asked: perhaps the human brain is, in some non-trivial sense, a digital computer? This is what brings us to the 'science' of artificial intelligence, and the work of Newell and Simon.

Newell and Simon

Despite their background in the social sciences, Newell and Simon are relevant to our story here for their work in artificial intelligence. A decade after Turing (in the 1950s) they worked on a number of highly important and influential computer programs: for example, Logic Theorist, the GPS (**G**eneral **P**roblem **S**olver) and SOAR (**S**tate, **O**perator **A**nd **R**esult). Now, obviously people had written computer programs before this, but Newell and Simon's work was different. They were attempting, consciously, to mimic *human* cognition on a digital computer. And, of course, this was based on a presupposition not just that computers could mimic human cognition, but that in some non-trivial way, human cognition *was the same as* computer 'cognition'. And this was because, allegedly, both the brain and the digital computer used algorithms (i.e. computer programs), which proceed in a deterministic, step by step fashion. For reasons that will become obvious later on, this belief is now, somewhat ironically, sometimes referred to as GOFAI, that is, Good Old Fashioned Artificial Intelligence.

It's worthwhile going back to see what Newell and Simon actually wrote because their views are a good deal clearer, more explicit, and more controversial than most of their successors: and it's important to state, yet again, that it is Newell and Simon's work which is held up to be the basis on which the computational theory of mind is built, which is, in turn (according to Pinker) the 'backbone' of EP.

'The theory' (they proclaim in their classic text *Human Problem Solving*, and by 'the' theory they mean 'their' theory) 'proclaims man to be an information processing system, at least when he is solving problems … the theory posits a set of processes or mechanisms that produce the behaviour of the thinking human. Thus the theory is reductionistic' (Newell and Simon, 1972: 9). Earlier on they make this more explicit: 'The present theory views a human as a processor of information. Both of these notions (information and processing) are long-established, highly general concepts. Thus the label could be thought vacuous, unless the phrase information processing took on an additional technical meaning. One may try to provide this by saying that a computer is an instance of an information processor'. (ibid). Now (and this is extremely important): many cognitive scientists (especially since the late 1980s for reasons we will explore later) tend to be a bit cagey about the extent to which they literally believe that the brain/mind is like a digital computer, generally stating things such as 'well it's just a metaphor' or something similar.

It's well worth noting that Newell and Simon reject this.

'Metaphors have their own good place in science … (but) an information processing theory is not restricted to stating generalities about Man. With a model of an information processing system, it becomes meaningful to represent in some detail a particular man at work on a particular task. Such a representation is *no metaphor* …' (emphasis added). (Newell and Simon, 1972: 5). Therefore, Newell and

Simon (and therefore, anyone who bases their own work on theirs, such as Pinker) are making an extremely strong claim: that the human brain *literally* functions, in some non-trivial way, as a digital computer (or, at least as a Turing machine). (As we saw, Turing also rejected the 'it's all just a metaphor' idea).

There's another point they make that is both important and true. To repeat: 'The present theory views a human as a processor of information ... Both of these notions (information and processing) are long-established, highly general concepts. Thus the label could be thought vacuous, *unless the phrase information processing took on an additional technical meaning*' (emphasis added). What they are pointing out here is that there is an 'ordinary language' use of the words 'information' and 'processing', which, as they point out is *not* the same as the scientific definitions of these words. In this 'common or garden' use of the phrase, it is, indeed, vacuous. In this definition, information merely means 'stuff that we know' and processing merely means 'thinking'. And it is in this sense that the phrase 'the brain is an information processor' is self-evidently true, and, as Newell and Simon point out, equally self-evidently vacuous.

In order to make the phrase 'the brain is an information processor' a *scientific thesis* (that is, one that tells us something which we did not know before: i.e. which explains something, and also one which is theoretically falsifiable [i.e. either true or false]) a technical, scientific definition of the phrase 'information processor' will self-evidently have to be produced. We will return to this point later.

Methodology

There's one other point that needs to be stressed here, although it is invariably passed over in an embarrassed silence by successor texts in cognitive science. If you read the vast majority of experiments as they are written up in the 'official' psychology journals, you will usually discover some little bit at the end that says something similar to 'results were significant (p<.05)' or 'results were found to be significant (p<.01)'. There's no room here to go into what that means (However: cf Wallace and Ross, 2006). But the key point is that these are the results of what is termed 'tests of statistical significance' (hence the acronym NHST: Null Hypothesis Statistical Testing), and that they define probabilities (the 'p' in the sentences above mean 'probability').

We are now going to have to make an extremely brief detour into the philosophy of science, but it's enough here to note that in the early 20th century, scientists were thrown into confusion by the development of the new science of statistics. Statistics dealt with the behaviour of aggregates of units (atoms, molecules, whatever) as opposed to the behaviour of individual units, and the laws of statistics were *probabilistic* as opposed to being *deterministic*. This was confusing to many scientists because, since Newton, scientists had assumed that it was their job to produce (or, as Newton would have it, discover) *deterministic* laws that predict how *every* object under consideration will behave. But probabilistic laws aren't of this sort: instead they give a *probability* that *most* things will behave in a certain way (Krüger *et al.*, 1987).

By the time Newell and Simon were writing, however, most scientists had come round to accepting that reality really was statistical, not deterministic, and the use of 'p values' demonstrated this. Therefore tests of significance are now a reputable tool to use in psychology. But, remarkably, Newell and Simon reject this view.[4] Instead, as they explicitly state: 'The reversal of the usual emphasis (i.e. on the analysis of aggregates of behaviour, described probabilistically) gives the present theory a quite distinct flavour. Thus individual differences is not a topic that is tacked on to the main body of our theory. On the contrary we never use grouped data to test the theory if we can help it ... it does not seem natural to

4 Interestingly, Skinner and the other behaviourists agreed with them, as they, too, were looking for deterministic, not stochastic laws of human behaviour. The continuities between cognitivism and behaviourism will be one of the themes of this chapter.

assume that human behaviour is fundamentally stochastic[5] ...
Freud's dictum that all behaviour is *caused* seems the natural
one ...' (Newell and Simon, 1972: 10). (emphasis added).
Indeed as their heading on page 13 puts it, their version of
cognitivism is a 'non-statistical theory'.

BUT (and this point is ignored by almost every one of
their successors) Newell and Simon are fully aware that
*you cannot infer deterministic, causal laws from the probabilistic
framework that underpins the 'classic' psychology experiment*
(which uses Null Hypothesis Statistical Testing [NHST],
to produce P values). Instead as they write: 'we employ little
experimental design ... experiments of the classic sort are
only rarely useful. It becomes essential to get enough data
about each individual subject'. Experiments, paradoxically,
don't really work if you want to infer deterministic laws
from them, because by definition they deal in aggregate
behaviour (i.e. the behaviour of *most* things). Now, and again
this shows the links between the early cognitivists and the
behaviourists (and for that matter, Freudian psycho-analysis),
Skinner *et al.* had also distrusted statistical tests for precisely
the same reason: he wanted to infer objective deterministic
scientific laws of behaviour, and, as discussed, you can't
really do that if your basic tools are probabilistic. Skinner
had nevertheless carried out experiments, but instead of
experiments on humans, he had carried out experiments on
animals.

The main reason for this is simple: animals are a lot less
complex than humans. Therefore, reasoned Skinner *et al.*: one
might be able to look at human behaviour in, so to speak,
microcosm. We can look at rats and pigeons etc. work out the
deterministic laws that apply to them and then see if they
'scale up' to humans. It may well be that *human* behaviour is
so complex that it can only really be described in stochastic
terms, but at least we'll know that that's merely a measure
of our own epistemological shortcomings: humans, are, after
all, merely a fancy kind of animal. So the basic deterministic
framework can be sustained.

---

5 Stochastic is another word for probabilistic.

But this pathway was closed to the cognitivists. Because cognitivists were and are interested in biological cognition *only insofar as it resembles the 'cognition' of a digital computer.* The extent to which any biological organism resembles a computer is moot, but it's clear that human behaviour resembles it a lot closer than any animal, if for no other reason than that computers 'talk': they can 'communicate with each other' and we can 'communicate' with them via computer languages. No animal has language.

Therefore the cognitivists couldn't really use statistics, but they couldn't use 'simple' experiments on animals either, as Skinner had.

So what did they have left? As Newell and Simon put it: '(that's why we are) emphasising the use of verbal behaviour as data ... thus the analysis of *verbal protocols* is a typical technique for verifying the theory ...' (ibid, p12).

Newell and Simon are interested in human beings, in a non-experimental way, but are not interested in human physical behaviour. By definition, therefore, they were forced to use human linguistic behaviour as data, because that's all that's left. But what are verbal protocols? Well as a quick glance of the appendices in which the data is presented shows, verbal protocols are simply transcriptions of what subjects said they were thinking when performing tasks.

In other words, not just in terms of its initial core beliefs, but in terms of its methodology, cognitivism is in many ways *structuralism's return* (or revenge). Certainly it is a far more complex theory, and it has the 'twist' of the computer hypothesis (*not* metaphor). Nevertheless, like structuralism, cognitivism claims to show the mental structures that we all share, and demonstrates their existence by simply asking people what they are thinking when faced with stimulus.

This helps to explain, I think, the hostility the cognitivists had to the behaviourists: it mirrored (and was, I think, partly caused by) the hostility the behaviourists had shown to the structuralists. They were both fighting over the same turf.

However, the point to be made here is all the thousands (perhaps tens of thousands) of psychologists who use NHST to attempt to infer deterministic 'cognitive' laws are simply using the wrong tools for the job (as Newell and Simon would have been the first to point out): Does this call into question the results of all the 'findings' of cognitivism which are based on NHST? Unfortunately, the answer is yes. Even more unfortunately, since Newell and Simon, almost all the evidence that is produced which allegedly supports cognitivism is based on NHST (The rest is based on 'verbal protocols', but the basic issue of reproducibility that destroyed structuralism has not been solved: instead it has been brushed under the carpet. Cf Nisbett and Wilson, 1977).

More connotations of Newell and Simon's theory

Another corollary of the rejection of 'group processes' and 'stochasticism' in favour of the individual and determinism, is that Newell and Simon's theories explicitly and necessarily rule out consideration of human beings as *social* animals. Indeed, they provide this as an even more fundamental reason for the rejection of experiments: almost by definition experiments measure the responses of human beings as they react to the stimulus of another human being or an object: whereas Verbal Protocol Analysis is a way of 'listening in' on human beings as they (effectively) *talk to themselves.*[6] This isn't all that Newell and Simon reject. They also reject consideration of 'sensory and motor skills' (i.e. walking, running, sitting, driving a car, engaging in any form of physical activity, looking, talking, listening, touching ... and so on), because, as they note, 'motor skills seem in considerable part to be non-symbolic' (ibid, p8). They also ignore 'motivational and personality variables': it should be noted that 'emotion' is counted as a 'personality variable' (ibid, ... p8). The reader

---

6 Strangely, the emphasis on verbal, qualitative data cannot fail but to remind one of psycho-analysis. Needless to say, behaviourism, (mainstream) psycho-analysis and cognitivism are united in seeing the *individual* as being the main 'unit of analysis' for psychology.

should remember this when we come to Chapter Seven, and the rise of the 'new psychology'.

Cognitivism

So then: what is the essence of cognitivism? Newell and Simon have gone to great length to say what it is *not*. But what is it?

Well it's very simple. Cognitivism is the belief that 'cognition' (or at least, some of it) is the action of *rules* (algorithms) acting on *symbols*.

As Pinker states:

> At the highest level of cognition, where we consciously plod through steps and invoke **rules** we learned in school or discovered ourselves, the mind is something like a production system, with **symbolic** inscriptions in memory... (Pinker, 2003: 112).

Therefore idea of the brain/mind as being something like a 'symbolic architecture' with rules (conceptualised as algorithms, similar to or identical to the algorithms in computer programs) is the essence of the cognitive approach.

Marvin Minsky

We'll move on to the other originators of Cognitivism in the next chapter, but we'll make one last stop here in the 'computer science' department, so to speak. Another name mentioned by Pinker in terms of the creation of the cognitive 'revolution' is Marvin Minsky. Again, Minsky worked in artificial intelligence, and generally speaking shared the views of others in the cognitivist 'revolution', but he's worth mentioning here for another reason: his early opposition to the theory of 'perceptrons'. Perceptrons were an early attempt at what we would now term a 'connectionist' 'neural network', and had been quite popular as a research theme until Minsky, with Seymour Papert, wrote 'Perceptrons; an introduction to computational geometry' in 1969. Attribution is doubtful at this late date, and to be fair, Minsky denies the charge, but it's likely that this work helped to create a sense of hostility to connectionist research that persisted until the publication of McClelland and Rumelhart's *Parallel Distributed Processing: Explorations in the Microstructure of Cognition* in 1986. The publication Minsky's paper at this crucial time ensured that funding for connectionism stopped dead in the '70s and early '80s (the high point of cognitivism) and that, therefore, it was the *symbolic* 'version' of cognitivism (i.e. the idea that cognition consisted of the operation of rules on representations, not the slightly more complex 'brain based' ideas of connectionism) that became the basic framework within which almost all psychologists worked between roughly 1970 and 1985. What's important to realise here is that at the time, the EPers were being taught basic cog-sci, the Minsky rejection of connectionism still held, and symbolic cognitive science and symbolic AI were considered to be the only games in town. Steve Pinker's hostility towards (or patronising condescension towards) connectionism should be seen in this context.

There are two more thinkers that Pinker mentions: Jerry Fodor and Hilary Putnam but we'll leave a discussion of them to later on in the next chapter when we look at the philosophical school of functionalism.

But the key point is that, as we saw right at the very beginning of this chapter, EP bases its view of thought, language and behaviour on cognitivism. According to EP, we evolved cognitive modules. But not for the present. Instead, these cognitive modules (or cognitive apparatus, or cognitive structures) arose for the Neolithic savannahs, in Africa. And, since, these cognitive modules are relatively 'static' (like the equivalent 'modules' in a digital computer, i.e. not 'plastic') we are, to a greater or lesser extent, 'stuck with them'. So whereas the question for sociobiology was: how do our current actions evolve, from an evolutionary perspective? EP asks, how did our cognitive architecture evolve to fit the environment of the Africa of (roughly) 50,000BC? And this explains the differences in methodologies between the two theories. Whereas sociobiology looks for 'matches' between modern behaviour and evolution, EP looks for *mis*matches: because, we are, according to EP, 'not at home' in the modern world. We evolved for Africa, we are stuck with that cognitive architecture, our capacity to learn or change is strictly circumscribed, and that is that. The distal cause of our behaviour is evolution, but the proximal cause are the cognitive algorithmic mental structures that evolved for Africa, all those years ago

But there is more to cognitivism than this. We have to look at the 'philosophy' of cognitivism before we have finally answered the question 'what is it?' But before then, let's look at the theorising of the linguist Noam Chomsky, who first led the cognitivists to believe that the mind might be 'modular'.

Chapter Two

Chomsky

One of the key assumptions of EP is that the mind is modular, and the evidence for this hypothesis derives, to a very great extent, from the theories of Noam Chomsky. So now let's look at Chomsky's theories. To be specific, as this is a book on EP, let's look at Chomsky's ideas insofar as they have influenced Steven Pinker and, hence, the EP tradition as a whole.

Pinker began as a cognitive psychologist, getting his PhD in experimental psychology at Harvard. Nonetheless his first books were mainly on the subject of linguistics (with the exception of *Visual Cognition,* 1985) : *Language Learnability and Language Development* (1984) *Connections and Symbols* (1988) *Learnability and Cognition: The Acquisition of Argument Structure* (1989) *Lexical and Conceptual Semantics* (1992).

Now in these books, Pinker takes over his basic theorising from the theories of Chomsky, who has provided one of the key bedrocks of the cognitive 'revolution'. What is important here is not just as one might expect, that Chomsky provided evidence that the mind works by processing internal representations via algorithmic rules: as we have seen, this was the key insight that founded the bedrock for cognitivism. But Chomsky went further than this by arguing that we are born with a Language Acquiring Device, a certain section of the mind/brain devoted wholly to language. In this LAD were 'stored' the basic rules that, for example, help us to decide whether a sentence is grammatical or not.

This is one of the key insights of cognitivism, in that it suggested that the mind/brain might contain modules: specific information processing subsections devoted to specific tasks. It was the philosopher Jerry Fodor, however, who really ran with this idea. In his key book *The Modularity of Mind* (1983) Fodor took Chomsky's ideas and developed them in order to argue that many, perhaps most, functions of the mind did not derive from general purpose 'holistic' faculties (as the behaviourists had argued), but were instead, produced from internal, discrete mental modules devoted to specific tasks. Even more than the idea of rules and representations this was the idea that really laid the groundwork for EP (although make no mistake, EP relies on the concept of rules and representations to 'work').

But we are getting way ahead of ourselves. First we should look at Chomsky's theories, then Pinker's use of them. And then, finally, we could look at whether or not this whole apparatus holds together.

Chomsky's Linguistics Revolution

In 1957 B.F. Skinner made a big mistake. Despite not being trained as a linguist, having any qualifications in it, or having done (much) empirical work in linguistics, he nevertheless published *Verbal Behaviour* (Skinner, 1991). This was an almost entirely theoretical book which attempted to apply behaviourism to linguistics. It was the publication of this work, which provoked a famous (or infamous) review by Noam Chomsky (in the journal *Language*, in 1959). This review immediately made Chomsky (in)famous, at least in linguistics, given the degree of vehemence with which he attacked Skinner's work, and not just Skinner's work in particular, but the whole behaviourist tradition in general. Chomsky loathed behaviourism for a wide variety of reasons (some philosophical, some scientific, but some moral) and was keen to see its hegemony undermined. (Chomsky, 1967)

Chomsky's review was 'right' insofar as it attacked Skinner's over-simplistic view of language acquisition and use. But it is one thing to claim that Skinner's views were wrong. It is quite another thing to claim that because Skinner was wrong that Chomsky's own views are therefore correct. This is particularly important as Chomsky's views were and (most non-linguists will be surprised to hear) *still are* highly controversial in linguistics.

However, the reasons that Chomsky's views became popular in the 1950s and 1960s will quickly become obvious when we look at the essence of Chomskyan linguistics which is his emphasis on what Chomsky himself entitled one of his own books: *Rules and Representations* (Chomsky, 1980). Or, to be more precise, rules acting on (internal) representations.

If this sounds like a theory of linguistics that is highly amenable to a cognitivist interpretation it's because it is. Indeed it was Chomsky's emphasis on the necessity of 'internal' modular information processing mechanisms (it's not often enough noted that Chomsky used the phrase 'information processing' to describe cognition, Lachman and Butterfield, 1979) as well as his emphasis on mathematical formalism that provided one of the key foundations of the cognitivist 'revolution'. (Boden, 2006)

Chomsky has had an enormous influence on modern cognitive psychology. This might seem peculiar since he is a linguist, but Chomsky's theories fitted the zeitgeist perfectly, and were interpreted (and over-interpreted) to provide the basis for a whole new way of looking at the human brain.

But the key point that must be grasped here is that Chomsky reacted against previous linguists who had emphasised that categorisation and classification were the essence of linguistics (Moore and Carling, 1982): which is to say, the classification of language in terms of surface features. Instead Chomsky emphasised that a genuine science of linguistics could only arise if linguistics were to look beneath the apparent chaos of language (and it is very important in Chomsky's view that this chaos IS only apparent) and perceive and then study the structure or structures that lie 'behind' this chaos. And Chomsky went on to argue (or rather, to assume) that these structures took the 'form' of, or could easily be modelled and described by, mathematical logic (at the time of Chomsky's initial writings, mathematisation was still seen as the holy grail for any aspiring science: cognitivism has taken over this love of quantitative data and suspicion of qualitative data). Given these views we shouldn't therefore be surprised that Chomsky became one of the key thinkers of the Cognitive Revolution.

So, Chomsky went about attempting to 'refound' linguistics, this time as the study of the timeless 'forms' or 'structures' that lie 'behind' or 'underneath' written and spoken language. And therefore Chomsky isolated the aspects of language that he thought lent themselves to this approach. This led him to look more closely at grammar. Grammar had up until the 1950s been generally seen as a grim and turgid subject, and to be honest, it's not a subject that makes many peoples hearts swell with excitement even nowadays. But most people before Chomsky had looked at grammar either in a classificatory way (i.e. they assumed that the task of linguistics was simply to describe and then classify all the various forms of grammar of all the languages of the world) or else prescriptive (describing how people 'ought' to write and speak).

Chomsky was after something very different. It occurred to him that, whereas the elements of language that were related to meaning would always be context bound, and would, therefore vary according to the situation, whether something was grammatical or not did *not* so vary. Moreover, there was little 'grey' about this distinction. Sentences were either grammatical or they were not. Again, this 'black or white' aspect of the distinction was attractive to someone who wished to model linguistics on mathematical logic: in the 1950s 'fuzzy' and dialetheistic logic were in their infancy and mathematicians and logicians were suspicious of 'qualitative' thinking: 'binary' thinking (yes/no for example, or 'one' 'zero') was much more popular (and it was also attractive that the language of artificial intelligence was the language of binary code).

However, in order to abstract grammar out of the 'flow' (or chaos) of everyday language Chomsky had to demonstrate that this could actually be done: i.e. that syntax (grammar) was different from semantics (meaning): otherwise the whole enterprise would be doomed from the start. This was the point of his famous sentence: 'Colourless Green Ideas Sleep Furiously' which attempted to show that a sentence could be perfectly *grammatical* whilst still being *meaningless*. Therefore grammar (syntax) could be studied as an 'isolated' system, independent of semantics.

Once Chomsky had demonstrated that this was possible, at least to his own satisfaction, he was then driven, so to speak, to posit the idea that 'underneath' all the various grammars of the world, there was 'one' grammar that was programmed into the human brain at birth. What reasons did he provide for this position?

We will look at the deeper reasons later on. However, for the moment it's enough to say that of course it was the *behaviourists* who had stressed the concept of the brain as being a learning device. And Chomsky, as we have seen, abhorred behaviourism. So he was driven to de-emphasise the extent to which the brain could learn things, and, given that people clearly know stuff, if you don't think they know stuff because they've learned it, you are driven to posit the idea that they must have been *born* knowing it, and that's therefore where Chomsky begins. And if we are all (or almost all) of us born with something it must be a human Universal, in the same sense that having two eyes or two legs is a human Universal.

And so based on these assumptions Chomsky was led to argue that the 'grammar' deciding or grammar creating 'aspect' of the human brain was something we were born with and was therefore a Universal. And then Chomsky went on to theorise that this 'aspect' of the human brain was 'localised' in a specific area of the mind/brain: hence his theory of a Language Acquiring Device (LAD).

It should be noted in passing that little or none of this was original. The idea that there was a 'Universal Grammar', went back to English Platonists of the 17th century, as Chomsky himself admitted (Chomsky, 1966). And the idea that various cognitive features are localised in specific parts of the brain was a mainstay of the 18th and 19th century pseudo-science of phrenology. (Fodor's subtitle to his best known book is less frequently quoted: the full title is 'Modularity of Mind: an Essay on Faculty Psychology', and, as Fodor admits in the first page, 'faculty psychology' is a phrase commonly associated with phrenology).

But again, one could say this about cognitivism generally. As with Cognitivism, though, the innovative aspect of Chomsky's work was not the substance of what he was saying, but the way he translated these ideas out of the language of 19th century biology or 17th century philosophy, and into the new language of mathematical logic and information theory.

We will look at the precise nature of the LAD later on. But what is of interest here is, to repeat, Chomsky's resuscitation of the ideas of phrenology. Phrenology had been abandoned in the early 20th century for two reasons, one trivial, one profound. The trivial reason was that phrenology was absurd: it posited the idea that the various 'areas' of the brain that were devoted to (say) language, or the aesthetic sense, or whatever, manifested themselves in the shape of the skull, and that phrenologists could therefore make predictions about people's cognitive capabilities by feeling their skulls. (Francis, 2004). By the 1950s this was felt to be all very silly.

But there was a more profound reason that phrenology was rejected, and we have already touched on it. It was because phrenology was implicitly or explicitly a nativist theory. 19th century psychology was very strongly deterministic and very strongly biased in favour of the idea that biological constraints influenced behaviour, and, therefore, biased *against* the idea of environmental influences. The inference was frequently drawn, therefore, that we are born with various cognitive faculties located in specific areas of the brain, that we die with them, and that little or no changes take place in the interim.

The reasons phrenology became popular in this environment should be self-evident.

But it was precisely these assumptions that the behaviourists rejected. With their lack of interest in what went on in the 'black box' and their emphasis on environment and learning, the assumption was usually drawn that the brain was a holistic learning mechanism, and that cognition was not to any great extent reducible to discrete brain areas. Even if it was admitted this was possible, behaviourists tended to see this as something that arose due to environmental pressures (in the same way that if one exercises with dumb-bells one's arms will become more muscly, but one can't therefore assume that someone with muscly arms has a genetic predisposition to use dumb-bells).

It was this last assumption that Chomsky rejected. In his emphasis on the idea of a Language Acquiring Device, or to be clearer, a Language Acquiring Module, he went back to the nativist/phrenological assumptions of the 19th century, or the even older theories of the 17th century Rationalists (especially, of course, Descartes). According to Chomsky we were *born* with a Language Acquiring Module, located in a specific part of the mind/brain, which came pre-programmed, so to speak, with information about (for example) what constituted a grammatical sentence.

And it was this idea, of the mind being modular, that the Cognitivists ran with. After all, they reasoned, if the mind contained one information processing module, dealing with language, then who was to say that it didn't contain many information processing modules? Indeed, perhaps cognition might be more of a matter of the various modules interacting with each other, as opposed to some form of 'holistic' thinking involving the whole brain?

Functionalism and Modularity

This brings us neatly to the final major influence on Cognitivism (at least according to Steven Pinker): the philosophical theory of functionalism. Functionalism is the idea that, to quote Levin: the function 'of a mental state [is] to be determined by its causal relations to sensory stimulations, other mental states, and behaviour.' (Levin, 2009). In other words: mental states cause behaviour. It's fairly clear why this might appeal to the cognitivists, and this becomes clearer when one finds out that functionalists promoted the idea of 'multiple reliability' which, when one cut through the rhetoric, implicitly or explicitly compared mental states to software (as opposed to the 'hardware' of the brain). Functionalism was a theory in philosophy which arose in the 1950s and was strongly associated with the philosopher Hilary Putnam: Jerry Fodor was also associated with the 'movement' although the extent to which he would describe himself as a functionalist is unclear.[1]

Be that as it may, it was Jerry Fodor who wrote one of the key books of Cognitivism: *The Modularity of Mind* (1983). This proposed that certain aspects of the mind could be described in terms of its 'cognitive architecture' and that this cognitive architecture could be described in terms of information processing modules. Although, as Fodor points out, in some ways his own theories are not the same as Chomsky's they certainly derive from them in non-trivial ways. And in his introduction Fodor also makes clear that his battles are Chomsky's: both of them were fighting the 'empiricist' (read: behaviourist) mainstream.

The Cognitive Revolution

Let's recap. In the 1960s there were four main 'strands' of thought that went to make up the so-called 'cognitive revolution'. The first of these was the development of the idea that cognition *just is* the manipulation of rules by symbols.

---

1 Fodor himself was sometimes characterised as a 'representationalist' instead, and was sometimes even seen as being anti-functionalist. But he clearly had quite a lot in common with the movement.

This is 'psychological cognitivism' proper. The second, very closely associated with this theory, is the project of what has been termed 'Good Old Fashioned Artificial Intelligence' (GOFAI), or, more accurately, 'symbolic' or 'classical' artificial intelligence (Newell and Simon). Thirdly there is Chomskyan linguistics. And finally there is the philosophical theory of functionalism which is very, very, similar to (some would argue, identical with) the theory of the Computational Theory of Mind (CTM) (most strongly associated with Turing, but also Newell and Simon), which is, obviously, the philosophical wing, so to speak, of GOFAI (given that the CTM is the theory that the mind is, in some non-trivial sense, comparable to a digital computer, albeit in an abstract form: i.e. a Turing machine).

If this seems complicated, it's because it is. One of the problems with arguing against cognitivism is that it has no acknowledge 'spokesman': a Skinner or Watson figure who is the 'public face' of cognitivism. Nonetheless, all these strands have tendencies in common, although, of course, individual thinkers may reject aspects of these ideas, or propose some elements more strongly than others. Nonetheless there are a number of features that I would argue are common to all or most of these schools of thought. These are:

1. The idea that cognition is similar to or identical to the use of rules or algorithms.
2. The idea that these rules/algorithms act on 'internal' representations (internal meaning, in internal 'cognitive' space). (Note: just to be clear, a 'representation' is, as the name suggests, a 'picture' or 'image' of an 'external' object. So an internal representation of a dog would be a picture or representation of a dog stored, somehow, in my brain). So in this view, memory is the act of using algorithms to retrieve representations from a memory store.
3. The idea that the mind is modular. The basics of this idea were developed by Noam Chomsky (who had the basic idea of a Language Acquiring Device, which, apparently, 'we' are all born with), although it was developed by the

philosopher Jerry Fodor in his work *The Modularity of Mind*. Modules, it is alleged, are 'domain specific computational mechanisms': domain specific meaning simply that they do one specific thing. So, for example, the proposed Language Acquring Device deals only with the grammatical rules of whatever language we happen to be learning. Modularity flowed partly from Chomsky's distaste for behaviourism (as we will remember, the behaviourists thought the brain was a holistic, general, learning device) but also partly from Chomsky's distaste for the empiricist tradition in general, in favour of the philosophical position of Rationalism, especially that aspect of Rationalism which descended from Descartes (we will return to this point later).

4. The idea that, in some non-trivial sense, the brain is similar to, or identical to, a digital computer. Note: this does not necessarily mean digital computers similar to the one I am typing this statement on now (although it may do). But it does mean that the brain is, in some abstract sense, similar to, or identical to, *an abstract model* of a digital computer (for example, a Turing Machine).

However there is one, so to speak, hidden influence on the 'information processing' view of cognition, who is rarely cited in the literature, although his definition of 'information' is absolutely crucial in terms of getting the whole theoretical superstructure off the ground. It is to this thinker we must now turn.

Chapter Three

Information Processing Theory

To recap: we have identified four major streams that fed into the cognitivist 'river'. One was from computing science, and descended from Alan Turing, uncoincidentally, also the founding father of Artificial Intelligence.[1] Second we had insights from management theory, based on Verbal Protocol Analysis, from Newell and Simon. Third we had the philosophical tradition of 'functionalism', of whom the most famous proponents are/were Fodor and Putnam, although nowadays the reputation of Daniel Dennett may well have eclipsed theirs. And, finally we had the innovations in linguistics brought about by Noam Chomsky.

But there's one interesting precursor of cognitivism that Pinker does not mention, which is strange. If the reader will cast his or her mind back s/he will remember a brief discussion by Newell and Simon as to why information processing, *without a rigorous scientific definition of that phrase*, would be merely a 'vacuous' theory. And this is obviously, and self-evidently correct: unless you know what is meant by the phrase 'information processing' the discussion as to whether

---

1 There was also an input from Marvin Minsky.

or not the brain 'is' or 'is not' an information processor can't even get started. Luckily such a definition exists. It was provided by Claude Shannon in the 1940s and it is to his work that we should now turn.

Shannon

Claude Shannon is the founding father of the science of information theory in that his paper 'A Mathematical Theory of Communication' (Shannon, 1948), essentially founded the field. It should be stressed here that regardless of whether or not it is admitted, ALL uses of the word 'information' in psychology (i.e. the scientific use of the word 'information') derive, ultimately, from Shannon.

This is not to say that there are not other uses of the word in science (the phrase 'Fisher information' is used in statistics, and the word has a relatively clearly defined use in physics[2]) but in terms of *talking about communication between human beings*, *all* uses of the word can be traced back to Shannon. In other words, the question 'is the brain an information processor', in a scientific context, is really the question 'is Claude Shannon's definition of information useful in terms of providing an accurate description of the actions of the brain'? What Shannon's theories are, therefore, is a question of no small importance to psychologists.

And yet, when one reads his original papers, why this should be the case is not entirely obvious. It's not pointed out frequently enough in psychology that Shannon was not, strictly speaking, a 'scientist' (i.e. not an academic, tenured scientist working in a University). Instead he was an engineer, working in the field of telephony. This is not to slight his work: Shannon was clearly a genius and his work has been massively influential. But it does indicate that the purpose of

---

2 There are links between these uses of information but they need not concern us here. The key point is that it is Shannon's use of the word that is pre-eminent in psychology.

his enquiry was perhaps, slightly different to what many of those who talk about 'information processing' often presume. To be specific, he was not a 'pure' scientist attempting to create timeless, 'Platonic' definitions of what information 'really is'.

On the contrary. Shannon's paper was an attempt to solve a specific problem: how to calculate what size of cable and how many cables it would be necessary to use in order to create an efficient and effective telephonic system for a given population. In order to do this, Shannon had to work out a measure of 'size' in this particular context: specifically he had to create an 'objective' measure of the 'amount' of communications that would have to be carried over the cables so that these could then be related to the capacity of the cables themselves (in order to make sure the cables weren't 'overloaded').

The solution Shannon developed (he was developing ideas previously discussed by other engineers like Nyquist and Hartley) was to provide an 'objective' measure of information: it could then be calculated what the information capacity of the proposed telephonic system would have to be.

So: what was Shannon's definition of information? Remember: this is the definition that ALL of the 'information processing' revolution relies on.

Shannon defined information as having the following aspects:

- An information source
- A transmitter
- A signal
- A receiver, which transforms the signal back into the message intended for delivery, and
- A destination. (Shannon, 1948).

He also invented the term 'bit' to define a unit of information, and, finally, defined 'entropy' as the measure of uncertainty in a message (in other words the degree of uncertainty caused to the receiver by the absence of a certain number of bits).

Shannon also made one extremely important point about

his own definition of information which is worth quoting here in full.

> 'The fundamental problem of communication is that of reproducing at one point either exactly or approximately a message selected at another point ... the significant aspect is that the actual message is selected from a set of possible messages. The system must be designed to operate for each possible selection, not just the one which will actually be chosen since this is unknown at the time of design. If the number of messages in the set is finite, then this number or any monotonic function of this number can be regarded as a measure of the information produced when one message is chosen from the set, *all choices being equally likely*' (Shannon, 1948: 379).

We will return to this point later, but the key point to grasp here is that Shannon defined information with such rigour that it gave us not only the basis of modern information science but also the beginnings of a new way of looking at cognition. After all, natural language (i.e. the spoken language we use every day) is clearly a form of communication... perhaps, therefore, it might be seen as a way of transmitting information? Pursuing this thought (thought cognitive scientists) perhaps the transmission of information is the *key purpose* of language ... and by the same logic, all the senses. In other words, looking at things from this perspective, the eyes receive information from the outside world via light waves, the ears via sound waves, the mouth *produces* information via sound waves, and so on. And this led to an even more momentous thought: perhaps, therefore, the brain was really nothing more than a mechanism for dealing with ('processing') this incoming and outgoing 'information'. And again, by analogy, this would highlight the similarities between the brain as information processor and the digital computer as information processor, because, obviously, this is what digital computers do: they process information from 'outside', that is, information made available via the internet, via the user, via DVDs and compact disk, and then, having processed it, produces it for 'transmission' in the form of output. So, for example, we 'input' information to a pocket calculator (say 'what's 2 plus 2') it 'processes' this, and then transmits an 'output' ('4'). Obviously the brain is far more complex, as is the information inputted and outputted. But perhaps essentially the same process is going on?

How and Why

We now have an answer to two questions: what is 'cognitivism' and, 'what is the information processing view of cognition'. Cognitivism is the view that the brain 'works' via algorithms, acting on representations in internal cognitive 'space', which is either the same as, or very similar to, the way that digital computers work, or at least, the way that abstract descriptions of the way digital computers should work, when seen as Turing machines. 'Information processing' is the idea that the brain processes *information* as that word is defined by Shannon.

We now have the 'How'. But what we are left with is the 'why'? Why did the early cognitivists wish to see the brain in this way? What led them to think that this was a good idea? And why did the EPers follow them in this belief? Clearly it is this last question that is particularly important for this book. Luckily, the answer is quite easy to find if we return to the key founding text of EP: *The Adapted Mind*. This is quite a long quote but it's important, as this defines what Evolutionary Psychologists were really trying to do in setting up their new science. (It's from Chapter One, the Psychological Foundations of Culture).

> *Disciplines such as astronomy, physics, geology and biology* have developed a robust combination of logical coherent, causal description, explanatory power and testability, and have become examples of how reliable and deeply satisfactory human knowledge can become ... this development is only an

acceleration of the process of conceptual unification that has been built up since the renaissance ... *the rise of computers and, in their wake,* modern cognitive science, completed the conceptual unification of the mental and physical worlds, by showing how physical systems can embody information and meaning. The design and construction of artificial computational systems is only a few decades old, but already such systems parallel in a modest way cognitive processes ...these intellectual advances transported the living, the mental and the human ... into the scientifically analyzable landscape of causation (Barkow, Cosmides and Tooby, 1992: 19–20) (emphasis added: note how the rise of cognitive science is, in this description, assumed to have been *caused by* the rise of the digital computer).

This, therefore, is the reason for the 'cognitive revolution' and, therefore EP. It is the quest, in other words, to produce a 'real' science of psychology, a science of psychology that would be analogous with the sciences of physics, chemistry, and so forth.

It's important to understand that this is a very old quest. Indeed it really goes back to Descartes and, before him, the scientists of the Renaissance, such as Galileo ('this development is only an acceleration of the process of conceptual unification that has been built up *since the renaissance*'). For this 'conceptual unification' is really the quest for the unification of all the sciences, in a 'web' of causality, with 'big causes' ('caused by' the laws of physics), leading down, at the end, to the smaller causes or causal factors leading to cognition. And it is also a dream that this will be accomplished via the mathematisation of all the sciences. This has been described as 'Descartes' Dream' (Davis and Hersh, 1987) (Descartes being the French Rationalist philosopher who Chomsky draws on so much), although the 'unification of all the sciences' was also an ambition of nineteenth century positivism. And as we saw, it is this belief, or ideology, that the world consists, 'really' of simple causal laws, that led to Turing inferring that therefore the world of cognition must also consist of simple causal laws: hence, algorithms. Hence the brain is a digital computer (or something very similar to a digital computer).

It is not a coincidence that cognitivism, which 'buys into' this idea, is often termed Cartesian (a word meaning 'in the tradition of Descartes').

Now it's rather ironic, and, to be fair, the logic is different and the conclusions are very different, but in essence the cognitivist dream is not really very different from the behaviourists' dream. Skinner and Watson, too, wanted to put psychology on a 'genuinely' scientific basis. In this sense at least, the cognitivists (and EP) are heirs to behaviourism.

But the question is: is the world really made up of simple causal laws? And even if it is does that necessarily mean that it is possible to integrate all the various 'worlds' of science? Is the idea that there is, or could be, a Theory of Everything meaningful? This issue goes back to Descartes, because it is Descartes who initially set up many of the distinctions that we now have to deal with when attempting to create psychology.

Now Descartes has had a bad press for the last fifty years, which is mainly because he is associated with Dualism, which, we are repeatedly told nowadays is a Very Bad Thing. (Dualism is the belief that there is physical stuff, which obeys mathematical causal laws, and mind stuff, which doesn't.) But it is less often discussed why he was forced, so to speak, to espouse dualism, and what this implied.

The fact is that Descartes was acting intelligently and in good faith, in the midst of a revolution, the so-called Scientific Revolution. There has been a huge amount of work in the history and sociology of this revolution that has cleared away much of the confusion with which it used to be surrounded. We now know, for example, that many of the so-called 'discoveries' of this revolution were not in fact discoveries at all, but had been previously known by the Chinese and the Muslims (for example Hobson, 2004): and, indeed, much of the 'Western' scientific method in fact derives ultimately from Muslim sources.

However that does not mean that the Scientific Revolution was not significant. It was. But what the Scientific Method produced was not so much new data as a new methodology, which was first proposed by Galileo, and then codified by Newton (Wallace *et al.*, 2007). The salient point here is the emphasis on causality and mathematisation.

During the Medieval period the reigning philosophy of science was Aristotelian. And Aristotle had a clear understanding of causality. His view of causality, however was rather different from our own, in that it included what we would now think of as 'meaning' and 'purpose'. For example, he divided causality into four aspects, and the fourth of these, 'the final cause' is the purpose for which something is done (Falcon, 2008). The view of causality that emerged out of the tumult of the Scientific Revolution, on the other hand, was different and much simpler. This new form of causality was bound up with the idea of determinism.[3]

In terms of the *new* causality, if X is the cause and Y is the effect, then, to say that X causes Y is to stated that there is a simple, determinist relationship between X and Y: i.e. X causes Y... always. And this facilitated the precision, or power, of the New Science. Never again would things be 'qualitative' or 'fuzzy' (stochastic). Instead scientific laws would be deterministic and, therefore, intensely powerful. As Francis Bacon remarked at the time: 'knowledge is power'. To know what the situation is at any given time, and to understand the causal laws that govern the phenomena in question might now give us total, deterministic knowledge of what will happen in the future: a heady goal. And it is this view of causality that Cosmides and Tooby are referring to when they speak of a 'scientifically analyzable landscape of causation '.

But the scientific revolution was about more than this. It was also about describing objects that were simple, and which had not only a causal, deterministic but also a *mathematical* relationship to each other (i.e. a relationship which could be described in terms of mathematics, usually in the form of

---

3 I am of course skating over highly complex issues here, hence the 'weasel phrase' 'bound up with' ... It's true that determinism and causality were not, precisely, the same ... But for the purposes of this argument it doesn't really matter.

mathematical 'laws'). Galileo wrote 'The great *book of nature* can be read only by those who know the *language* in which it was *written*. And this *language* is *mathematics*.' (Quoted in Devlin, 2003 emphasis added).

This leads to a third point: that the elements that are being linked together here in a 'causal chain' (that is, a simple, deterministic, causal relationship) are themselves simple (geometric): i.e they are like squares or circles. And this leads to the final point: that the degree of prediction and control of these elements is dependent on the extent to which they function 'ceteris paribus' (i.e. all other things being equal). Or, in other words, the extent to which they function free of context.

It's often been pointed out how amazing it is that the laws of Newton, for example, function so well in outer space, such that the movement of spacecraft, etc. can be predicted with such high levels of precision millions of miles away. But actually that's precisely where we would expect such levels of precision to be possible. Because in space there are no (or few) 'confounds' that interfere with our laws: no atmosphere, wind, effects of weather, rain etc.. The situation in space tends to be pretty simple: you have objects moving around in empty space, and in these situations, the laws of (e.g.) Newton function pretty well (except in unusual circumstances where we need the laws of Einstein as well).

But on Earth we have more complicated factors, which is the reason that when we talk about prediction of objects, we are really talking about the precise prediction of the behaviour of *mathematical idealisations of objects*, not (really) the objects themselves. On Earth, the experiments rarely 'turn out right' as some of us will remember from school science classes (Cartwright, 1999).

Newton's View of Science

And this is the view of science that Cosmides and Tooby

are discussing when they talk about the degree of progress made by the 'hard' sciences as opposed to the so-called 'soft' sciences. In other words (just to be crystal clear about this) they are setting up at the beginning, criteria for the 'success' or 'failure' of a science, and then stating that *by these criteria* the soft sciences have been a failure. But of course, the 'success' of the methodology of the hard sciences was made possible by the fact that the objects under discussion *were amenable to this form of analysis*. Planets, comets and spacecraft can be discussed as if they are simple geometric objects that engage in simple causal relationships with each other (even though they actually aren't, this doesn't really affect the accuracy of the predictions).

So a perfectly reasonable conclusion to draw from the success of the hard sciences is that we should choose the tools that match the task: in other words, that the success or otherwise of a science will depend on whether or not the appropriate methodologies were chosen. But that's not, of course, the conclusion that Cosmides and Tooby (and others) drew. Instead they drew the conclusion that the methodology of the 'soft' sciences should mimic that of the hard sciences.[4] But this might be a problematic assumption for all sorts of reasons.

Galileo on Primary and Secondary Qualities

Cartesian dualism has, as noted, attracted a great deal of criticism. But it's the 'primary-secondary qualities' distinction that I want to deal with here. This was first clearly stated by the English philosopher John Locke, but it's implicit in the theorising of Galileo and Descartes.

---

4 It should also be noted that this desire to 'map' psychology onto Newtonian physics presupposes that the cognitive modules that exist in the human brain are all pretty much the same, in the same way that electrons (etc.) are all pretty much the same. And this is necessary to demonstrate the simply causal laws which govern human behaviour. Involving context would make things too difficult and would rob the laws of their deterministic nature.

The problem, for these early scientists, was how to set out an area of science that they could deal with. So they chose their area of study to match their presupposed methodology (not the other way round, as is generally assumed). Now there's no real room to go into the whys and wherefores here, but, very briefly, Galileo was strongly influenced, not just by mathematics per se, but by the Platonism that was coming to replace Aristotelianism, as the dominant philosophy of the time. And this posited mathematics as the 'true' language of reality (and by mathematics, of course, as we have seen, Galileo meant geometry). Hence, objects that were amenable to being 'geometry', so to speak, were designated as being Galileo's object of study: hence, primary. Everything else, which wouldn't really 'fit', so to speak, was 'secondary'. Or as Galileo put it:

> I believe that nothing is required in external bodies except shapes, numbers, and slow or rapid movements. I think that if ears, tongues, and noses were removed, *shapes and numbers and motions would remain,* but not odors or tastes or sounds. The latter I believe are nothing more than names when separated from living beings, just as tickling and titillation are nothing but names in the absence of such things as noses and armpits. (Galilei, 2007: 52–53). (emphasis added)

Now of course it was precisely 'shapes and numbers and motions' that Galileo was interested in. As a purely pragmatic distinction, to be made by a working scientist, this is fair enough. But the problem comes when one accepts this as a truth statement about the world. Because then we end up in a situation where only the objects of 'natural science' are considered to be actually *real*. And this is highly important because it's from this distinction that we derive another distinction so important to philosophers and scientists in the 'West': between the Subject and the Object. If we remember anything about Descartes it's his thought experiment where he speculates about how he really knows anything. Perhaps he is being misled by an all powerful demon?

Descartes concludes that ultimately all he really knows is that he is a thinking conscious being: and that CAN'T be doubted. Therefore: Cogito Ergo Sum: I think therefore I am.

But this view privileged, to a very great extent, the thinking conscious mind, now seen as being literally the fount of all knowledge. In drawing a distinction between the world of 'external' objects, and the world of thinking 'internal' subjects Descartes was also making another distinction, between 'subjective' 'internal' thoughts and beliefs and 'objective' 'external' phenomena. This follows, although by no means clearly, from Descartes' scepticism, and relies (in ways we don't have time to go into here) on Descartes' theology. 'Within the Meditations themselves, the chief epistemic principle is that which maintains – partly on theological grounds – that "whatever I clearly and distinctly perceive is true." In Descartes's scientific practice, this effectively meant that epistemically warranted scientific claims *must* be framed mathematically' (emphasis added) (Broughton and Carriero, 2007: 502). Moving swiftly past the question of whether Descartes' ideas really make sense here,[5] suffice to say, Descartes was left to hypothesise a geometrical world, extended in space, which was 'out there', open to mathematical analysis and 'objective' and opposed this to an inner world that was 'subjective'.

However, as Alan Costall puts it:

> Few psychologists really appreciate the fundamental role that subject-object dualism played in the rise of classical physical science.

---

5 Descartes' theorising really depends on his theology here, which is why, one might argue, attempts to 'secularise' or describe Cartesianism in a materialist framework don't really make sense. The whole point of the 'Demon' is that everything in the 'outside' world might be an illusion. But Descartes wants to give the truths of geometry 'objectivity'. He is therefore driven to posit mathematics as being God-given, and he has to do this, or else he would be lost in a world of solipsism.

The remarkable successes of the new physical science – its wide application to the 'heavens', to earthly events, and even to the understanding of the human body – encouraged its proponents to make highly ambitious claims on its behalf. Thus, according to Descartes, the new physics was nothing less than an all-embracing science of nature. However, the implication of this claim was that anything failing to figure within that science *must exist beyond the realm of the natural* (Wilson, 1980, pp. 41–42).

Despite all of his solitary cogitation, Descartes was not acting alone. Galileo and Kepler, among many others, also engaged in a similar 'ontological fix' to save the universal claims of the new physics (Burtt, 1969; Whitehead, 1926; Young, 1966). Their general line was that the new science was in the business of explaining *everything* – and hence anything the new science failed to explain was not *really* real. Within this scheme, therefore, psychology's eventual subject became radically subjectivized, as that which *eludes* scientific methods. As Alexandre Koyré put it:

'[Modern science] broke down the barriers that separated the heavens and the earth. [But] it did this by substituting for our world of quality and sense perception, the world in which we live, and love, and die, another world – the world of quantity, of reified geometry, a world in which, though there is a place for everything, there is no place for man' (Koyré, 1965: 24).

Classical science 'set up' psychology to be a very odd kind of enterprise. Once physical science had promoted its methodology (of atomism, mechanism, and quantification) to the status of an exclusive ontology, psychology was a pretty obvious mistake just waiting to be made, a science that would take on the awkward residue of the 'subjective' which classical science had already defined in opposition to the 'objective'. (Costall, 2007: 167–168)

Ignore the bits about the subject–object distinction for the moment. What we are looking at here are the basic assumptions of the Scientific Revolution. What we see here is nothing less than the birth of what we now call Scientism. To repeat, there is absolutely nothing wrong with what Galileo etc. were propounding and in their own terms, it all made perfect sense. What went wrong with it was their universalising tendencies. It was quite one thing to claim that the methodologies that were being developed for the Hard Sciences were the best methodologies for the subject under discussion. It was quite another to claim that these methodologies were the only ones that were valid, and that, in fact, any alternative methodologies *weren't 'really' scientific*.

It's clear that once one creates these dichotomies (the 'subject-object' distinction so very important to Western science, from which we get the idea of things being either 'subjective' or 'objective', and the 'internal-external' distinction, with objective phenomena being related to 'external' phenomena and 'subjective' to 'internal' … the new world of 'inner space' being created and then, so to speak, rendered mysterious by the new physics) then a genuine scientific psychology is not only 'odd' but actually a contradiction in terms. Because psychology, is by definition, what is 'inside' and 'subjective'… which is, again by definition, the 'stuff' that *isn't* scientific and which *can't* be looked at via the scientific method.

This is an extremely important point and we must remember it when we hear (as we have done so many times over the last 150 years) that psychology 'must' become more scientific (more like Galilean or Newtonian physics, in other words). This is what Watson proclaimed, and then Skinner, and then Chomsky, and now the EPers, always claiming that the failures of their predecessors were due to their being insufficiently 'scientific'. Looked at from outside this game, however, we can identify the problem as being far more fundamental. The reason that psychology has not made the 'progress' made by physics, is that, simply, within this framework, *it can't*, because, to repeat, a genuinely scientific psychology (i.e. one following in the Cartesian tradition) is simply a contradiction in terms. It can't be done, and it is safe to say that, given that minds of the calibre of Watson, Skinner, Chomsky, Freud, Wundt, Seligman etc. have not succeeded in creating such a science that no one else will succeed either, not in ten years and not in a thousand.

For the dark secret of Western psychology and philosophy is that, for four hundred years, with a few exceptions, philosophers and psychologists have agreed about a lot more than they have disagreed about. It's not as if the arguments between Rationalists and Empiricists and Freudians and behaviourists are not real. They are. But there are hidden assumptions that *frame* these debates. To see what these assumptions are we have to look at the implications of the Scientific Revolution for philosophy.

Representations

In philosophy there are what are generally termed the 'Big Questions'. Who are we? Where are we going? What is the Good Life? And so forth. But perhaps the biggest question of all is What is Truth? Before the scientific revolution there had been quite a lot of answers to that question, going back to Plato (we will return to this point). But with the Scientific Revolution, new answers to this question became possible, and these answers still hold many (Western) philosophers in their sway. The question is 'what is truth' and the new twist on the question was that we now have a distinction between 'inner' and 'outer' experience, with, always ticking away at the back of our minds, the idea that we should try and be as much like physicists (that is, theoretical physicists using mathematics) as possible. So, if we accept these assumptions it becomes almost impossible not to conceptualise 'internal' 'cognitive' objects as behaving more or less like physical objects: i.e. like the sort of physical objects analysed by physicists. And then we have a solution to our problem. We have 'internal' objects, which are 'geometrical'. But we also have 'external' objects, which are also geometrical. What, therefore is truth? In this view: something is true if the internal object 'maps onto' the external object: in other word, if it **represents** the external object accurately. So say I am looking at a square object: say, a square table. Is it true to say I am looking at a table? Well, in this view, the answer is 'yes' if my 'internal representation' of a table 'matches' or 'maps onto' the external table.

But this then leaves us with another problem. If we conceptualise these internal objects as being (essentially) physical: what moves them about? In the external world, it is the rules or laws of physics, apparently, which moves things about. What about our 'internal' representations? What moves them? The obvious answer is that there 'must be' internal 'rules of thought' (analogous to the laws of physics) to 'move' our cognitions about, so to speak. And then, of course, given that we are living in a digital world, it's easy to start seeing similarities between these 'rules of cognition' and the (apparently similar) rules or laws of cognition (algorithms) which 'power' digital computers.

So we now have a working model of cognition as well as of truth. As Noam Chomsky put it as the title of one of his books: cognition consists of 'Rules and Representations' or, to be more clear, cognition 'is' rules *acting on* representations, and something is true if an internal representation 'maps onto' an external object. And even to those who do not go this far, the distinctions between inner and outer, subjective and objective are still too tempting to let go of.

This is the hidden belief system that unites even those who appear to oppose it: Kant and Hume, Bertrand Russell and Sigmund Freud. Even the behaviourists, who appear to reject the 'inner' and 'outer' distinction in fact do not do so (Heft, 2001).

Rules and Representations

In order to become a theory of truth, this theory, of rules acting on representations, becomes not just a theory of psychology, as we have seen, and a theory of epistemology (what we can know) but, as well as this, a theory of ontology, a theory of what is, in fact, the case.

Because then we have a total theory: if we start to conceptualise reality as consisting of discrete, geometrical objects, relating to each other via causal deterministic laws (ontology) then we can also say that the way in which human beings interact with this world is via internal algorithmic laws, internal rules, interacting causally with internal geometric type objects (which is epistemology, but also a theory of psychology) and that something is 'true' if these internal objects 'match up to' the external objects. This belief system or philosophy is called Realism (with a capital R) and despite what is often implied in the basic cognitivist texts, it is NOT to be confused with common or garden realism which is the idea that a mind independent world exists. The philosopher Hilary Putnam has called this representational view 'metaphysical realism' to make this point clearer.

It's going too far to say that this theory reached it's apogee in the philosopher Ludwig Wittgenstein's work *Tractatus Logic-Philosophicus* (published 1922). Going too far because there are certain elements of this world picture (especially the elements that attempt to derive a theory of psychology from Newtonian physics) that are very far from Wittgenstein's own views. Nevertheless, Wittgenstein's theory of truth (the so-called *picture theory of truth*) and the resulting theory of representationalist psychology was, perhaps, stated most clearly in the *Tractatus*. And the influence of this book was vast: on the logical positivists, and via them, to the theories of physics, metaphysics, and psychology prevalent in the 1950s, the period in which the basic tenets of cognitivism were first stated.

However, I have argued elsewhere (Wallace *et al.*, 2007) that this view really derives from the origins of Western thought: from the writings of Plato. It was Plato who originated Western Rationalism, and it was Plato who (taking this view over from Pythagoras) stressed that mathematics was the way to 'touch' the Real that lies outside space and time. Plato's views (speculations) were overtly metaphysical as opposed to the covertly metaphysical views of the Metaphysical Realists, but essentially there's not much difference: in both views the goal of philosophy/science is to 'match' our internal representations to external mathematical forms.

So, to repeat, and to state this in the clearest possible way. The cognitivists, and, then, evolutionary psychologists were forced to adopt a certain way of looking at psychology and a certain way of doing things because, from their own point of view they had no choice. If you wanted to make progress, then you had to adopt the dualist/Cartesian worldviews, because that seemed to be the only way to do science. But the cognitivists were wrong.

Quantum Mechanics

Frequently, reference is made to the 'scientific method' as though there is just the one. But this is false. There is no one, single, scientific method. How could there be? Science includes not just physics and chemistry, but botany, earth science, astrophysics, ecology, systems science etc. Then there are the applied sciences, like medicine, engineering, psychiatry, and architecture ('building science'). And this is without even discussing the human sciences, mathematics and computer science, assuming one accepts that these are true sciences. But by what criteria could we make that decision? The only way we could do that was to decide, *a priori*, that certain sciences were 'real' and others aren't. But how do we do that?

The fact is that there are debates and discussion in all sciences, even about absolutely fundamental issues, like what constitutes science, and what is truth in a scientific context? The one debate I want to talk about here is the debate between Einstein and Bohr in the 20th century, not only to demonstrate that there are disagreements even in the alleged 'high priest' of the sciences, theoretical physics, but to demonstrate just how fundamental these debates can be.

There have been numerous discussions about the debates between Einstein and Bohr, but the key point here is that Einstein was a Realist in the sense above. In other words, he saw the point of science as being to make truth statements about the world, and by truth statements he meant mathematisations (or mathematical idealisation) of the causal deterministic laws that governed the behaviour of all matter and forces in the Cosmos.

Bohr did not believe this, as was demonstrated by his view of the Copenhagen Interpretation of Quantum Mechanics (note; it has been pointed out that many people had and have different interpretations of this Copenhagen interpretation and that, for example, Heisenberg saw it a bit differently from Bohr. So for the purposes of simplicity I'm just going to stick to Bohr's views).

There are two fundamental differences between Bohr and Einstein. To repeat, Einstein was a realist. He believed in causality, in determinism and the Truth of science. Bohr on the other hand 'believed' in none of these things, at least in terms of quantum mechanics. Instead he was an instrumentalist. **Instrumentalism** is the view that concepts and theories are useful instruments whose worth is measured not by whether the concepts and theories are true or false but by how effective they are in explaining and predicting phenomena.

Writers on quantum mechanics have frequently confused this issue by continually attempting to drag the Copenhagen Interpretation into a Realist framework by talking as if Bohr was attempting to make statements about what is or what is not the case.

For example the famous examples of Schrödinger's cat, or the fact that a particle 'is' a wave or a particle, are not, as is generally stated, questions about what is, or is not, the case. To take the first of these examples. Briefly, this is a 'thought' (not a 'real') experiment, in which a cat is put in a mechanism which kills it if/when an electron decays. The electron decays (or doesn't), and so the cat is either killed (or not). But since, according to QM, we do not know whether or not the electron has decayed before it is measured, unless we actually open up the mechanism and take a look we don't know if the cat is alive or dead. This normally leads to the statement that until we measure the electron (or open the cat killing mechanism) the cat is neither 'alive' nor 'dead' but in some other state of 'dead-aliveness'. But the fact is that Bohr believed with Wittgenstein that 'whereof one cannot speak one must remain silent'. Yeah ok, if you insist: from some Platonic 'birds eye' view we could 'find out' whether or not the cat was alive and whether or not the electron decayed. But Bohr's point was that it is that since we cannot, by definition, have this 'birds eye' view, it is meaningless (not false, but *meaningless)* to ask these questions. This is not Idealism. We do not 'conjure' the cat out of the air when we 'measure it', but what is the case is that *there are no meaningful answers* to the question about what's in the box and whether 'it's' a wave or a particle before we measure it.

To put this into layman's terms: Bohr's answer to the question: 'is the cat dead or alive before we measure (i.e. look at) it (or the electron)', is 'Well, how the hell should I know? And, frankly, who cares?'. The Copenhagen interpretation is not about Truth in an absolute sense, it's about what we *can* know. And in this case, we can't know whether or not the cat is alive or dead and it's pointless to ask. The Copenhagen Interpretation of QM is not a theory of ontology, it's a theory of epistemology (for the very good reason that in this view a theory of ontology is a contradiction in terms. It's meaningless to ask 'what exists' without asking 'and how can we measure/ observe what exists') (Faye, 2008).

Now it's obvious that if you adopt this viewpoint that questions about truth become less important. Therefore, as well, since we have abandoned the idea that the idealised mathematical world (which is 'external') is 'True' (or even that this statement means anything) then we no longer have the problem of how this is 'represented' via internal schemas or representations. Instead we move towards a theory, not of what is true, but of what is useful: and this moves us towards pragmatism.

Interestingly enough, it also moves us towards positivism. 19th century positivism stressed very strongly the importance of mathematics, and it's this that cognitivism picked up on (as did QM: QM is a highly mathematical theory). But positivism *also* stressed a high degree of scepticism towards unobservable entities and metaphysical truth claims, which, unfortunately, cognitivism did NOT pick up on. For example, Stephen Hawking once wrote, about Roger Penrose, who we shall meet again: '(Roger) is a Platonist and I'm a positivist. He's worried that Schrödinger's cat is in a quantum state where it is half alive and half dead. He feels that can't correspond to reality. But that doesn't bother me. I don't demand that a theory correspond to reality ... all I'm concerned with is that the theory should predict the results of measurements.' (Hawking and Penrose, 2000: 121)[6]

But of course, according to the Copenhagen Interpretation that's precisely what physics does: it creates useful fictions that predict experiments. It doesn't 'look behind' anything. So in this view, the idea that psychology *must be* the science that looks behind behaviour to see the mathematical/logical structures which correspond to it, in the same way that physics *must be* the science that looks beyond mere physical structures to see the Platonic, mathematical forms and truths that lie behind them, is false.

So to repeat: cognitivism arose because cognitivists made a choice as to how they wanted to 'run' their new science. They *chose* to model their new psychology on their understanding of Newtonian/Galilean physics, which predisposed them to adopting the assumptions of Descartes who was the key propagandist for this approach. It is simply not true that there was no alternative. However, once that choice was made, then cognitivism (or something very like it) became almost inevitable, and they were helped in this by their use of Shannon's information theory which seemed to give them a way of adopting a dualist approach that seemed not to be dualist by counterpointing the world of matter to the mysterious world of 'information'.

---

6 Note the use of the word 'correspond' in the above passage incidentally: Hawking is claiming that the idea of correspondence is intrinsic to Platonism: as we have seen, this idea is also stressed in the correspondence theory of truth, and cognitivism.

Shannon again

So let's now go back to Claude Shannon, and let's ask a question that very few cognitivists do: will his definition of information actually 'work' as a term in psychology?

To repeat what has just been stated: the cognitivists were obsessed with making psychology scientific, which meant, within the strictures they had set themselves, objective (mathematical, Platonic). This was the attraction of Shannon's theories. To state that human beings process information is merely 'vacuous'. However if one has a tight and objective, *mathematical,* way of defining information then this begins to sound like quite an enticing prospect, as it might then lead to an objective and mathematical way of defining *cognition.*

But will this work? Let's look again at Shannon's definition of information:

> The fundamental problem of communication is that of reproducing at one point either exactly or approximately a message selected at another point ... the significant aspect is that the actual message is selected from a set of possible messages. The system must be designed to operate for each possible selection, not just the one which will actually be chosen since this is unknown at the time of design. If the number of messages in the set is finite, then this number or any monotonic function of this number can be regarded as a measure of the information produced when one message is chosen from the set, *all choices being equally likely* (Shannon, 1948: 379).

Here Shannon makes two statements: 1: one can accurately measure the amount of information (the purpose of his investigation, remember) if, and only if, the number of possible messages is a finite number (obviously: you can't divide something by infinity) and 2: that all messages are equally likely. And by 'equally likely' what Shannon was getting at is that the content of the message was irrelevant, *because Shannon's definition of information has nothing to do with meaning.* On the contrary: it *can't* have anything to do with meaning, because otherwise it would make the measure of information too difficult. Shannon's theory is (intentionally and knowingly) homuncular: in other words, it presupposes that there are human beings who set up the telephonic system and who wish to communicate via it, in the same way that cognitivism presupposes that human beings build the computers and memory stores and algorithms etc. Or to make it even clearer: 'information processing' overtly (like cognitivism does covertly) presupposes (human) cognition. It does not and cannot explain it. And the reason is simple: Shannon is attempting to define information 'objectively'. If he introduces 'subjective' things (like meaning, specifically, what the information means) then he won't be able to do that.

But of course human communication *is* meaningful. The phrase 'information processing' has been wrenched out of its original context and then made to support a gigantic theory of cognition, something it was not meant to do and which it in fact cannot do. Human beings, communicate, yes, but they do not (in any *scientific* sense) process information. To quote Raymond Tallis: 'The engineer's use of the word information *cannot apply outside its legitimate provenance*: that of devices designed by human beings to help them communicate with other human beings'. (Tallis, 2004: 58). Nor will the defence of saying that 'we' are using the phrase 'metaphorically' work: the whole point of the definition is to create a non-metaphorical, objective definition of the word information. Either you are saying human beings literally and objectively process information or you aren't: no 'half way house' is possible.

However:

> From the early 1950s sensory perception began to be interpreted as the acquisition of information ... from this it was a short step to see perception as an (act of) information processing and to regard the function of the nervous system as that of transmitting information from one place to another (Tallis, 2004: 57).

The key phrase here is 'began to be interpreted'. To repeat:

like cognitivism, 'information processing' is not a discovery, like the discovery of the rings of Saturn or the discovery of the Komodo Dragon: the objective discovery of something that was previously unknown to science. Instead both cognitivism and the information processing view of cognition are best seen as interpretative acts: a way of 'joining together' various facts that were already known in a new way. And this decision was not forced upon psychologists by the evidence: instead choices were made (with no small amount of sociological influence) that led to psychologists *deciding* that these new ideas would facilitate interesting new research programmes.

These ideas were not forced upon psychologists by the evidence. Instead they were seen as means to an end: the end being to model psychology, as much as possible, on 17th and 18th century theoretical physics. And as we have seen, Evolutionary Psychology was motivated by the same desires. With its emphasis on mathematisation and objectivity, seeing perception and, then, cognition itself, as information processing seemed to meet these aims.

But it won't work because, to use the word information even in terms of communication (to repeat: its *only* valid use in this context) there would have to be a finite number of possible messages and each message would have to be as likely as any other. But neither of these criteria are met when talking about human beings. To begin with, as Chomsky, ironically enough, has been at pains to point out, human beings are creative, and there does not seem to be an upper limit on the 'amount' of sentences that people can come up with. For example Chomsky himself came up with the sentence 'Colourless Green Ideas Sleep Furiously'. No one had ever written such a sentence before. It might have stayed unwritten had Chomsky not written it. And, with the constant introduction of new words and phrases into the English (and other) languages, there is a constant new promise of novelty in the number of possible sentences we can use to communicate.

Neither are all sentences equally likely. If I walk up to you and hit you, you might say: 'what are you doing?' or 'stop that!' or 'If you keep on doing that, I'm going to hit you back, mate' or something similar. It's highly unlikely, on the other hand, that you will say 'Colourless Green Ideas Sleep Furiously' or 'My hovercraft is full of eels' or begin to recite the periodic table. This is because language is context specific, and certain uses of language are more appropriate than others, and this in turn follows from the fact that language is a method of establishing and communicating intersubjective *meanings*. If I was to tell you that my response to a question was 'fine thanks, how about you?' you would guess quickly that it is likely that the question being asked is 'how are you?' or something similar. And you can make this plausible guess because there are meaningful social norms that bind societies together via (amongst other things) language.

Therefore the most crushing argument against Shannon's use of 'information processing' as a metaphor or model for human communication or human perception is that both these phenomena are all about meaning, and Shannon's definition of information was purposefully designed to exclude meaning. So, if one is talking about Shannon's use of the word, *it is simply false to say that human beings transmit information in language.*

However, one might add that it is one thing to misuse the word 'information' to use it to refer to communication. This, whilst being illegitimate, is at least plausible. It is quite another to make the gigantic inference that just because this is the case (which it isn't) that therefore the purpose of the human brain is primarily or wholly to process information. And it is an even bigger logical leap to therefore assume that the brain *actually is* an information processor in the same sense that a digital computer is an information processor. This is a highly counter-intuitive claim, for which strong evidence would have to be provided. So: what evidence did the cognitivists provide for the 'digital computer' claim? It is this question that the next chapter will answer.

Chapter Four

So, we now understand what cognitivism is, and why it was adopted by the first scholars in the field of EP. The next question to be asked is: is it true? Is it in actual fact the case that the brain is a Turing machine? Is the mind modular? It is these questions that this chapter will attempt to answer.

AI and Cognitivism

At this point it's necessary to reiterate something that really shouldn't need any emphasis but somehow frequently gets forgotten: just how closely entwined 'good old fashioned artificial intelligence' (GOFAI) and cognitivism really were.

As Friesen and Feenberg put it:

> This basic idea of the reducibility of thought to formalized logical, mathematical or mechanical rules and processes lies at the heart of artificial intelligence. It is already explicit in the first definition for this field: Artificial intelligence is proposed as 'a study' proceeding from 'the conjecture that every aspect of learning or any other feature of intelligence can in principle be so precisely described that a machine can be made to simulate it' (McCarthy, *et al.* 1955).

This early conjecture has more recently taken the form of a scientific, experimental hypothesis *that has firmly linked artificial intelligence with cognitive science* generally (e.g. Sun, 1998). Simply put, this hypothesis is as follows: if thinking is indeed a form of mechanical calculation, then development of calculating machines (i.e. computers) has the potential to unlock the 'mathematical laws of human reasoning' posited in the West's Rationalistic tradition. ...

If thinking is information processing, in other words, then hypotheses about how we think can either be proven or falsified by being successfully 'modelled' – or by being proven intractable – through the development and testing of software systems. (Friesen and Feenberg, 2007, emphasis added).

This was the goal: to turn psychology into a 'true' science via computer models of cognition. But, equally, improved understanding of human cognition would help AI to model human cognition and therefore help to achieve AI's goals. A virtuous circle would then be achieved.

Now there was a very good reason for this interest in AI, which is that, apart from purely philosophical reasons (which by definition were always theoretical) cognitivists never precisely made clear why they thought the brain was a digital computer in any *scientific* sense: that is, they never made clear to what extent the idea that the brain=digital computer (or Turing machine) was a genuinely scientific hypothesis.

Now simply put like that, this might seem like a rather astonishing state of affairs. Compare the situation in other sciences for example. When a chemist states (for example) that water=H_2O or a physicist states that E=mc^2 two things are happening. Mysteries are solved (The mysteries being: what 'is' water? What 'is' energy?). Secondly the equals sign here really does function as an equals sign. A chemist *really is* claiming that water 'just is' H_2O, and a physicist *really is* claiming that an amount of energy really does amount to mass multiplied by the speed of light squared. Moreover, the relationship works both ways, so to speak. The first 'equation' tells us not only what water is, but what two molecules of hydrogen combined with one of oxygen, is. The second equation tells us not only that energy has mass but that mass is 'frozen' energy. *Moreover, for both these equations it can be proven that this is the case.* Simple electrolysis (i.e. passing an electric current) through a glass of water will produce hydrogen at the cathode and oxygen at the anode. The use of nuclear weapons, sadly, demonstrates that $E=mc^2$.

The 'equation' that 'the brain=a digital computer (or at least a Turing machine)' aspires to this level of precision but it's not at all clear it achieves it. To begin with, how would one go about *proving* it (in the same way that electrolysis and nuclear reactions prove the equations above)? The failure to answer this question clearly has led to a big problem for cognitivism. Then there's the second aspect of these equations: that they define both 'sides' of the equation. So if a brain 'just is' a digital computer, then presumably a Turing Machine really is a (conscious, human) brain, but hardly anyone believes this (actually like many of the claims of the 'cognitive revolution' it's not clear that this statement means anything).

However, to return to the first question: how would one go about proving that the brain is a Turing Machine? What is the analogous process to the 'electrolysis' process as used on water, above? There are only two options here: firstly, to 'decompose' or 'reduce' the brain: (i.e. to tear it apart and then demonstrate that it 'really' reduces to bits and information, just like a digital computer) or else to build a digital computer that functions just like a brain, and, therefore, because of the behaviours produced by both, (which presumably would be similar, or identical) conclude that 'really' they were the same.

Now it's clear that (via the H_2O analogy) the better way to prove that a brain is a digital computer would be to look at the brain, analyse it, chop it into smaller and smaller pieces (assuming that we are talking about a living brain, metaphorically speaking!) and then prove the brain/computer identity that way.

But, rather surprisingly, the early cognitivists did not do this. This seems counter-intuitive, but actually follows fairly logically, not from the nature of Western science, but from the nature of Western academia.

In the late 19th, early 20th century, it became obvious that new 'sciences' were going to become acceptable in Western universities, and that this meant there would therefore be new opportunities for lecturing (and other) posts. Moreover, whoever 'set up' these new subjects would immediately become known as the 'father of ...' (insert name of new science here).

And it was also clear that in order for this to happen, and to establish the 'serious' credentials of these subjects it would be extremely wise to stress the 'scientific' nature of these subjects. This was many, many, decades before post-modernism, and the sociology of scientific knowledge, and the sort of 'scientism' that has since become unfashionable was still very popular.

However this led to an interesting paradox. The philosophy of science that was popular at this time as we have seen was known as 'positivism' and one of the key tenets of positivism was 'reductionism'. What this meant in practice was that science was viewed as being a sort of pyramid with theoretical physics at the 'top', chemistry below it, and so on, down to the 'social sciences' at the bottom. And this was because of ideas first proposed by Descartes: specifically his idea of uniting all the sciences via a shared 'language' of mathematics (as we have seen, this has been termed Descartes' Dream).

However, by the late 19th century, when the social sciences were establishing themselves in the Western academic system it was not so much the unity, as the autonomy, of the various 'new' sciences that concerned scientists. For example, when Durkheim wrote *Rules of Sociological Method* (1895) he was very keen to stress the extent to which sociology was an autonomous science which could not be reduced to any other: and the reason for this was obvious. If sociology was an autonomous science then it would deserve its own faculty or department, its own professors and lecturers, and so forth. And this in a context in which many people doubted the validity of any form of social science, and argued that they would never attain the precision and accuracy of the 'real', 'hard' sciences. Durkheim, therefore, had his work cut out for him.

But if the position was difficult for sociology, it was even more complex for psychology. Because, for reasons we will look at more fully in Chapter Seven, the cognitivists accepted Descartes' view that cognition was 'really' all about brain states (in other words that so-called 'embodied' or 'social' aspects of cognition were less important ... as we have seen Newell and Simon also accepted this idea). But if one accepts this, it might well be argued, surely, if all thought 'came from' or was 'caused by' the brain, then surely all thought could, in theory, be 'reduced to' brain states. And this would mean that, in theory, the scientific study of psychology might become 'reduced' (or at least reducible) to 'neuro-psychology.'

This wasn't too much of a threat at the end of the 19th century, but by the mid 20th century with increased surgical knowledge, and (later on in the century) increasingly effective mechanisms of brain imaging (MRI and so forth), the threat became more and more apparent.

Ironically enough, the behaviourists had a solution to this problem, but due to their 'hard-line' approach, this was a solution that cognitivists simply could not use. The behaviourists response was simply to say that psychology was the science of behaviour, full stop, *not* thought or consciousness or whatever. Cognition could be indeed studied by brain scans, EEG readings and so forth, but behaviour in the 'real', 'physical' world would be the domain of psychology.

But of course, the cognitivists couldn't play that particular card, because cognition was precisely what they claimed to be explaining. And if the cognitive science could not maintain its position as an autonomous science, this would leave the possibility open that at some point it would be 'eaten up' so to speak, at some point in the future, by neuroscience.

So the way out of this dilemma was for the cognitivists to portray itself as a 'real' science, like physics, yes, but instead of being 'reducible to' biology (the most obvious choice) the cognitivists argued that cognitive science would instead be 'reducible to' computer science. So the 'reduction process' would go: Conscious thought (cognition), which is 'made up of' information, which reduces to information science, which in turn is instantiated on biological hardware which is then reducible to biology, and *then* physics. The autonomy of psychology (now reconceptualised as 'cognitive science') was thus preserved, but at a price, a price, which, to be fair, did not seem to be particularly high at the time. (See Fodor, 1974 for an early example of this approach).

The price was that psychology after the 'cognitive revolution' cut itself off from neuroscience, claiming that it 'didn't need it'. After all, assuming (and in retrospect, although this seems like a big assumption now, given the poor state of brain science at the time, it seemed plausible) that it was possible to 'run' a Turing type machine on biological hardware (i.e. the brain) but also possible to run the Turing type machine on *any* kind of hardware, then what difference did it make what specific form of hardware was involved? Cognitive scientists therefore saw themselves as being like software engineers. If there is a problem with Windows or Word or Excel you don't need to know anything about the computer hardware on which it's running to fix it. And so this is why, rather surprisingly one might think, philosophers like Jerry Fodor, who normally were (and are?) arch-materialists and reductionists, found themselves claiming that in this particular context, anti-reductionism was the way to go.

For, make no mistake about it, although in theory the cognitivists emphasised that, ultimately, the basic 'building blocks' of cognition (the 'ones' and 'zeros' of the world of information) were ultimately instantiated on the brain, and were, therefore, *ultimately* reducible to physics, in practice how this was to be accomplished was rarely, if ever, spelled out. Indeed, this glaring omission leads to the suspicion that there is a subtle kind of dualism going on here. There is, according to cognitivism, the 'world' of information (cognition) and then there is the 'world' of physics and material objects. The world of information is *ultimately* reducible to physics (we are told) but unless it is stated how this can be done, this ultimately functions as a kind of promissory note that is never cashed. It's as if the cognitivists said: 'Of course one *may* reduce the world of cognition to a material object' (in this case the brain) 'and I'll get round to telling you how this might be done in a few years time …'. But that time never came, and how this 'reduction' was to be accomplished was never explained.The air of dualism that hangs around this approach is something we will return to. But the key point is that this anti-reductionist stance (or at least anti-reductionism to physics) in the short term, removed the 'threat' to psychology posed by neuro-science.

So the cognitivists never tried to 'cut up' the brain to see if they could find bits (pun intended!) that looked like bits of a digital computer. But, if you don't go down the 'reductionist' road, what's left? The short answer is, not much … unless one accepts that GOFAI is an intrinsic part of cognitivism and is in fact the major support that holds the edifice up. Because this gives you a way out. One could argue all day and all night about whether or not the brain is 'really' a digital computer: and in fact since this was always a philosophical hypothesis (not a scientific one) that's what happened.

However if one could actually create a computer that could, to all intents and purposes, mimic human behaviour then this would render the whole argument moot. *So what* (cognitivists could say) if there was no scientific or quasi-mathematical proof that the brain was a digital computer. Here's walking, talking proof that it must be! And indeed this would seem to be a fairly strong argument. If there was a computer that could mimic human behaviour (or, indeed, cognitive processes) then surely there must be something in the brain=computer idea, and counter-arguments would start to sound churlish, or, indeed, desperate. And so Artificial Intelligence, at least in its GOFAI form, became an extremely large part of the cognitivist enterprise. If GOFAI succeeded, essentially, cognitivism would be justified.

Therefore it's extremely important to look at the roots of GOFAI, what happened to it, and whether or not it fulfilled its promise before we can properly evaluate cognitivism.

The Two Roots of GOFAI

We saw Pinker arguing in an earlier chapter that the 'roots' of cognitivism lie with Alan Turing. And, as we saw, Turing argued that because all material objects were subject to the laws of physics, therefore the brain must also be subject to these laws, and, therefore, thought or cognition must be describable in law like terms. He then made the logical leap of arguing that these 'laws of thought' were similar or identical to the algorithms of a digital computer. Therefore, the 'cognitive architecture' of any human being must be describable in algorithmic terms, and must therefore be implantable (so to speak) on a digital computer. There are a lot of assumptions here and we will go back and look at what is really being implied here later on. At the moment however, let's just go with this argument and see where it leads us.

Turing's argument was taken up and elaborated by a number of philosophers in the 1950s and 1960s who were mainly known as functionalists, as we have seen. Functionalism was a way of looking at the brain that, yet again, opposed itself to behaviourism, in that, unlike behaviourists, functionalists actually wanted to look 'behind' behaviour to 'look at' cognition itself.[1]

Therefore functionalists looked at mental states as autonomous, and argued that their significance lay not in their relationship to brain states, but in their relationship to other mental states, and, ultimately, behaviours. The key point about functionalism here is that mental states were meant to be 'multiply realisable' which meant that, in practice, 'where they were' wasn't so important as their relationships to each other. Or to put it even more simply, it didn't matter if a thought was lodged in a brain (so to speak) or a computer:

---

1 However, it is less often stressed that functionalism also opposed itself to another philosophy of mind popular at the time: 'eliminative materialism' or 'Type physicalism'. 'Eliminative materialism' which claimed, briefly that cognition *just is* brain states, would not leave any room for an *autonomous* science of psychology, instead, reducing psychology to biology and then physics. So the cognitivists rarely showed any interest in it.

what was important was its causal relationship with other thoughts and then behaviour.

What this meant, obviously, yet again, was that the question of whether or not the brain 'was' a computer was rendered moot: the question was: 'can human behaviour or cognition be represented on a computer'? And, theoretically, if one accepted functionalism, the answer, clearly, was yes.

We'll look at problems with functionalism in a little while, but here the key point is that Turing's point gets remade with a vengeance. Most of us are aware, however dimly, of the 'Turing Test' which is supposed to be a test of machine intelligence. What is supposed to happen is that a human (you, perhaps) is presented with two computer interfaces. One of them is attached (so to speak) to a human operator. The other one is really just a computer.

Turing's point was: when one comes to a situation where few or no human beings can tell the difference between the human operator and the computer operator, then who can say that the human is 'more intelligent' than the computer? In other words, Turing is attempting to render the question of whether or not the brain 'really is' like a digital computer meaningless. **If** a computer could mimic a human then, *to all intents and purposes*, a brain would have been shown to be like a digital computer and vice versa. Therefore GOFAI would have been justified, and, therefore, cognitivism would also have been shown to be have been justified. The key word here, of course, is 'if'.

The Proof of the Pudding

So: in the absence of a 'proof by neuroscience', success in the GOFAI enterprise was vital to prove that cognitivism was really a meaningful research programme. Before we go on to ask whether or not GOFAI really did succeed, it's worthwhile remembering exactly how confident the early AI pioneers were that not only was AI possible but that it would be achieved relatively quickly.

Herbert Simon: 'Machines will be capable, within twenty years, of doing any work a man can do' (Simon, 1965: 96).

Marvin Minsky: 'Within a generation ... the problem of creating "artificial intelligence" will substantially be solved' (Note: a 'generation' is normally defined as being, roughly, 30 to 40 years). (Minsky, 1967: 2).

These statements were written at the high point of GOFAI, and the birth of cognitivism proper, assuming one dates the inception of cognitivism to be identical with the publication of *Cognitive Psychology* written by Neisser in 1967. Needless to say, these predictions did not come true. Only 6 years after Neisser, in 1973, Professor Sir James Lighthill published the Lighthill Report, which concluded that 'Most workers in AI research and in related fields, confess to a pronounced feeling of disappointment in what has been achieved in the last twenty years ... in no part of the field (artificial intelligence) have discoveries made so far produced the major impact that was then promised'. (Lighthill, 2001: 505). Lighthill's report became a self-fulfilling prophecy in that it led to reduced public funding for AI which led to even less progress. In the United States, where science funding did and does tend to have a more military aspect, DARPA (Defence Advanced Research Projects Agency) cut back on AI spending, again in 1973–1974. This produced the first so-called AI winter, which was not helped by the publication of Hubert Dreyfus's *What Computers Can't Do* a book which we will turn to in later chapters.

However, AI bounced back, and by the late 'seventies, early 'eighties, funding resumed. This was the high point of cognitivism, and between 1980 and 1985, buoyed by the success of GOFAI, cognitivism and the 'information processing approach' to cognition really were the 'only game in town'. This was also the period, of course, in which EP was first formulated.[2]

---

2 They were helped by the death, in 1979, of J.J. Gibson, whose ecological psychology was perhaps the only major academic threat to the cognitivist orthodoxy. Concurrent attacks on psycho-analysis (the so-called Freud Wars) which erupted in the late '70s probably helped to ensure cognitivist hegemony as well.

Alas, this new wave of enthusiasm for AI suffered the same fate as the first. In 1987 funding for AI began to collapse again (not helped by the collapse of the 'Lisp Machine' market: Lisp was a computer language that was meant to have provided the bedrock for the new wave of artificial intelligence research, for example the Japanese Fifth Generation Computer Systems Approach). (Crevier, 1993) This time it was not to recover. The second, and much darker, AI Winter began in the 1990s and continues to this day. As of the time of writing this book (2010) the GOFAI project lies in ruins. Or, as a journalist surveying the contemporary scene has put it, GOFAI has 'over-promised and under-delivered'. (Markoff, 2005): The journalist also notes that, nowadays, serious researchers generally try and distance themselves from the AI 'label' as much as possible, due to its connotations of disastrous, humiliating failure.

Of course, it should not therefore be inferred that the money spent on AI was wasted. On the contrary, every time one switches on a PC, drives in one's car, or enters a modern building, one is taking advantage of the various technological breakthroughs facilitated by AI research over the last 40 years. But AI has become more successful by turning away from its original goal (to simulate human intelligence) and instead concentrating on useful gadgets that help human beings accomplish *their* goals. At the time of writing, the dream of creating the real life equivalent of Frankenstein's Monster, or The Golem, or HAL from the movie *2001: a Space Odyssey* is as far away as ever.

Chess and AI

GOFAI was a failure. Why it was a failure, is a question we will ask later. However, let's leave that to one side for the moment and ask a deeper question: what if, in the face of all the evidence, AI was to succeed at some distant point in the future? Even if *all* actions of the human brain were 'mimicable' by a computer, what exactly would that prove? And who would decide whether or not something really had been mimicked?

Take chess for example. For many decades, it was predicted that 'one day' computers would be able to play chess as well as humans (i.e. they would be able to 'mimic' human chess playing abilities). And for many decades nothing much happened. Scoffers scoffed, proponents of AI said 'one day …' and so it went on.

And then, in 1997, a purpose built IBM computer, 'Deep Blue' finally defeated the world champion, Gary Kasparov. Finally, it seemed that the machine had proven not only that it could match, but out-perform the best a human could do.

In the cold light of day, however, it is not clear precisely what this match proved, if anything. To begin with, the 'library' of games that Deep Blue used was of course provided by human grandmasters, and the computer was reprogrammed by a human grandmaster between games. The machine itself, of course, was built by humans. Kasparov was denied access to information about previous games that Deep Blue had played, although of course Deep Blue (or to be more precise, Deep Blue's human programmers) had access to all the games that Kasparov had played. In the game itself, the machine and Kasparov were more or less even for the first five games, until in game 6, Kasparov's game disintegrated: leaving Deep Blue the winner by 3 and a half games to 2 and a half. Without going into details (if only for legal reasons) Kasparov has consistently maintained that the 'behaviour' of Deep Blue was suspicious and that the possibility of human interference in its performance cannot be ruled out. The only way, he maintained (and maintains) to sort out the issue once and for all is to have a rematch: but IBM dismantled Deep Blue immediately after the match was over. (King, 1997)

Computers are good at chess. But what does this prove? Does it prove that computers are good at chess and therefore in the future they will be able to cognize in the same way human beings cognize? Or does it merely prove that we, in the 'West', for reasons of pure chance, happen to live in a society in which a game which lends itself to being played well by a computer is considered to be the supreme intellectual challenge? After all, in China and Japan, the equivalent game is *Go*, a game which computers are extremely bad at (although to be fair their performance has improved a bit in the last few decades).

In any case, even if we accept that Deep Blue 'won' against Kasparov, what does this prove? Kasparov lost because he panicked and because he suspected that the Deep Blue team was breaking the rules. In other words, he lost because he was a human being, and had emotions. Deep Blue won because it had no emotions and could not 'panic' (one could argue that when the computer crashed this might be the equivalent: but whereas when Kasparov 'crashed' in game six he was forced to concede, when Deep Blue crashed Kasparov allowed engineers to fix it). On the other hand, Kasparov, at the end of the game, knew he had lost. Deep Blue didn't know it had won , because Deep Blue, arguably, doesn't 'know' anything, if one is using that sentence to indicate the sort of knowledge that human beings have.

We are stuck with the problem: fishes swim, but do submarines? To make things clear: we sometimes talk about cars 'running' (as in 'the car's running well'). We don't actually mean that cars run in the same way that humans run. The metaphor is obvious in this example, but one could argue that 'the brain is like a digital computer' is just as metaphorical. It's not normally the case that, for example, in biology, we begin with an automated model version of an animal's behaviour and then look at the animal's behaviour in terms of the model we have created. For example we don't often encounter in biology textbooks, the sentence: 'in order to ask the question of why fishes swim, we must first look to a submarine, and *then* look at fish behaviour, but *only* insofar as this resemble the actions of a submarine'.

And even if we decided that submarines really do swim, is it valid to infer that, therefore, the mechanisms that 'drive' fish and submarines are the same (that fishes 'really' have propellers, engines, a crew etc.)? In other words, is it valid to infer even if a computer could pass the Turing test that therefore, *they cognize in the same way as humans* and that, therefore, humans cognize in the same way as computers? If

GOFAI succeeded it would be a huge triumph for GOFAI. But only if it were *proved* that GOFAI had succeeded by mimicking the 'internal cognitive mechanisms' of a *human* could *cognitivism* be justified.

So: to repeat, even if computers *were* able to replicate human behaviours it is not clear what that would prove. But of course, it has become obvious over the last few decades that computers can *not* mimic the vast majority of human 'intelligent' behaviours and that there is no reason, apart from blind faith, to think that they ever will.

So: AI was *not* a success. Why not?

What (Digital) Computers Can't Do

As we have seen, there are a large number of answers to this question. But one of the most important answers to this question was stated by the philosopher Hubert Dreyfus, in his classic *What Computers Can't Do*. In this book, Dreyfus argued that the problems that beset AI were not practical, as had been generally thought, but conceptual. Dreyfus argued that the main thinkers of AI were attempting to mimic, not human cognition per se, but their own view of what human cognition was. But argued Dreyfus, human beings do not, in fact, think that way. Moreover, it was impossible that human beings ever could think that way. So attempts to mimic human cognition via this 'traditional' or 'standard' way, (what become known as GOFAI) were doomed to failure.

And what Dreyfus predicted soon came to pass. There are an almost infinite number of ways in which GOFAI 'went wrong'. But some of the key problems it ran into are as follows.

1. The Qualification Problem. These problems are all related, and they stem from the cognitivist, GOFAI assumption that cognition is rule based. Say, for example, I, an electronic

'brain' get an order (in rule form, obviously) to build a boat and cross a large river. Now, how will 'I' know that I have met the criteria of 'having a boat'? When, in other words, will I know when to 'start my task'? This seems trivial but is not. For example, I need a boat, OK, but first I need to check that it doesn't have any holes in it. Then I have to check that it is, generally speaking, seaworthy, which means I have to check all the various ways in which a boat can be unseaworthy (and this already involves checking a very large 'nautical' database). Then I have to check that 'I' have 'everything I need': oars, safety equipment, compass, map, whatever else I need. Then I need to check that I know where I am going, that I can guide the boat well enough, that the river is not overflowing, that the weather is sufficient and so forth. And it should be noted that of all these features, there are other, ancillary features that need to be checked: 'checking the weather' involves knowing how to do this, knowing what weather is 'safe' and what is not, checking the safety equipment and so forth.

Very quickly, even for this relatively simple task, the amount of 'ancillary' data that has to be retrieved becomes extremely large indeed, and in a real world situation, contemporary computers simply do not have the processing power to accomplish even these apparently simple tasks. (McCarthy, 1996).

2. The Ramification problem. Whereas the qualification problem involves working out what needs to be done before something is done, the ramification problem involves working out what happens afterwards. Science fiction minded readers may remember Isaac Asimov's Three Laws or Robotics, which are: A robot may not injure a human being or, through inaction, allow a human being to come to harm. A robot must obey any orders given to it by human beings, except where such orders would conflict with the First Law. And finally, a robot must protect its own existence as long as such protection does not conflict

with the First or Second Law. The ramification problem involves how these would work in reality. Take a situation where a robot walks into a room and sees two men having a fight. Clearly the robot must stop the first man hitting the second. But this would involve force. The first man might get hurt. Moreover, say there is a third man in the room. The first man shouts out that the second was trying to hurt the third, and will surely succeed if the second is let free from his grip. Then, the third man, who is drunk, says 'no it's ok! I can take him!'. It's clear that the robot has an almost insoluble problem here, in that it would take gigantic memory and processing stores to work out what really 'is for the best'. But time is what the robot does not have. Again, in reality, with contemporary processing power, no modern computer or robot can solve these problems in anything like the timescale required (Papadakos, N. and Plexousakis, D., 2002).

3. The Frame Problem. The frame problem is put simply: what is or is not relevant to solving any given problem? Again, say I have to perform a normal life task like 'book a holiday'. What is or is not relevant to this task? I can get holiday information from virtually anywhere. Moreover I can book almost anyway I want. What should I do? Talk to friends? Read the papers? Read a book? Look up places on the internet? All of these things? What about if these data sources contradict each other? And what is and is not relevant? Should I buy geographical books? History books? Talk to friends/family about experiences? And so on. Again, here the problem is time. Given an infinite amount of time, then obviously the problem can be solved. The question is, how are these problems to be solved in real time situations? (McCarthy and Hayes, 1969).

If these problems sound similar it's because they are, and they all stem from one main situation: digital computers, with finite memory stores, having to retrieve algorithmic instructions to cope in a reasonable time frame with real world situations. Whereas, in theory, sometimes, some kind of 'solutions' to these problems can be found, in reality it has proven extremely difficult, or impossible, to mimic human behaviour in these situations: and yet human beings seem to manage it with ease.

Of course one could argue, and it has been argued, that the key point in this sentence is the phrase 'finite memory stores'. Perhaps, it is argued, far more complex and powerful memory stores in 'future' digital computers will be able to solve this problem. Perhaps. But equally we should at least consider the possibility that human beings 'solve' these problems by virtue of the fact that they do not in fact cognize in the same ways as digital computers. One must always remember here who is making the claim: the claim that at some (usually undetermined) point in the future digital computers 'may' or 'will' have computing power equivalent to a human is merely a claim, and an irrefutable one at that (therefore making its status as a *scientific* claim unclear). What *is* clear is that this argument is clearly 'special pleading' given that it is only ever used to avoid discussing the rather more salient fact that as of 2010 computers can clearly *not* mimic human intelligence in any meaningful way (*despite the fact that the founders of GOFAI clearly predicted that they would*). To reiterate what was stated in the introduction: the burden of proof that GOFAI might lead to 'human like' intelligence clearly lies on the *proponents* of that thesis, not on those who argue against it. Given that this is the case, the 'pro-GOFAI' argument, at the time of writing, clearly fails.

There are three major 'legs' of possible scientific support for cognitivism. The first is to actually look at the human brain and see how it works. As we have seen the cognitivists chose not to do that, and for good reasons, as we shall see. The second was the success of GOFAI. To put it very politely indeed, the jury is still out on the ultimate success of GOFAI. Suffice to say, as of 2010, there is no particular reason other than blind faith to think that GOFAI will succeed at any point in the next

30 or 40 years, given its failure over the last 40. This leaves us with logical, philosophical arguments for cognitivism. It is to these that we should now turn.

Chapter Five

Cognitivism arose as a reaction to behaviourism. And so, before we ask, is cognitivism true, we should, perhaps first ask: is behaviourism true? If not, why not? And if it's not true, then to what extent has cognitivism solved whatever problems that behaviourism ran into?

As noted before, most Psychology University Heads of Departments would rather see a burglar in their office than a behaviourist, so this might seem like a moot point. But actually it raises some interesting questions. There were, I would argue, three main strands to the behaviourist project.

1. Stimulus-Response (and subsequent elaborations) as the basic model for human behaviour.
2. Denial of 'inner' mental states.
3. The individual as being the basic level of analysis.

Of course it's number 2 that gets all the attention, but arguably this is to place emphasis in the wrong place. After all there were numerous kinds of behaviourism. It's true that Watson denied the existence of any and all 'inner states' but B. F. Skinner certainly *didn't*: he merely denied that they had a direct causal influence on behaviour which is a very different argument ('The objection to inner states is *not* that they do not exist, but that they are not relevant in a functional analysis' quoted in Modgil, 1987: 64). (emphasis added). Moreover, other kinds of behaviourism in fact *did* accept both that there were 'inner' mental states and that they could be causal but merely insisted on the principle of parsimony: that they should not be presupposed unless the evidence was overwhelming that such states existed.

It's worthwhile making this point (i.e. that behaviourists were not all barking mad, as cognitivists tend to imply) because, after all, it should not be forgotten that the behaviourists did actually have a point. It's not exactly irrelevant to mention that it's a bit weird to build an entire science on something that can't ever, under any circumstances, be observed. Cognitivists and others have attempted to blur this distinction by appealing to physicists, who posited electrons and so forth long before they could be observed. But (aside from the fact that such things now can be observed through electron microscopes etc.) even in the case of superstrings etc. there is no *theoretical or philosophical* reason as to why they can't be observed: merely pragmatic ones. It's true that (assuming that they exist) that superstrings can't be 'observed' by any conceivable technology or science. But that's not to say that in 100 or 1000 years such technology might not become available. This is very different from the situation with 'inner states', 'cognitive architecture' etc., which are alleged to be *philosophically* unviewable: we can never see them no matter *how* advanced our technology becomes.

So how do we know they are really there? There is one short answer and it is the only correct one: we don't. Cognitivists *posit and hypothesise* inner states, and *posit and hypothesise* what these states consist of: they have not in any sense *proved* that they exist, let alone that they have proved that they exist in the way that they (i.e. the cognitivists) claim that they exist (that is, even if one accepts the existence of mental states, one need not accept that these mental states are analogous to the software of a digital computer: Uttal 2000).[1] This is not to start

1 This is demonstrated by the uncomfortable fact, ignored in the texts of EP,

to defend behaviourism, let alone in it's 'radical' form. But it is to point out, yet again, that cognitivism arose from a desire (not a discovery), a desire to make psychology a 'hard science' like theoretical physics, and the *feeling* (one would not want to put it any more strongly than that) that information science, and the speculations of Turing might be a means to that end. This is, yet again, rather different from the scientific revolution of, say, Galileo. Galileo's 'new science' was indeed based on metaphysical assumptions, and the desire to 'remake' science, and put it on a firmer scientific footing. But it was also based on hard empirical evidence: Galileo's observations of the moons of Saturn. Cognitivism is not like this: it was not based on new evidence, new observations or new experiments. On the contrary: cognitivism is predicated on the idea that observations or *direct* experimental manipulation of the alleged 'cognitive architectures' etc. could never take place. Instead it was based solely on abstract theorisation by Turing and, later on, the 'functionalists', qualitative interviews carried out by Newell and Simon, and work on artificial intelligence.[2]

Now, the key issue here is that when behaviourism was popular, it was widely derided (or at least disliked). But it was not disliked because it denied 'inner states'. Instead it was disliked because it seemed to give us a highly reduced, determinist and degrading view of ourselves, as being merely 'rats' *who reacted to stimulus.* Behaviourism, after all, was intended to be the science of 'prediction and control'.

But, it cannot be stressed enough that this part of behaviourism, i.e. the bit that stressed stimulus-response (which was, in turn, taken over directly from the cause-effect metaphor from Newton) *was unchanged in cognitivism*

---

that behaviourism has not gone away, and recently has looked as if it may be making a slight comeback. Interested readers may wish to check up on the Association of Behaviour Analysis (http://www.abainternational.org/) which currently has 5000 members, a number which is growing.

2 As well as, of course, the ideas of Noam Chomsky. But those who have not read Chomsky are sometimes surprised to see how theoretical and un-empirical his writings are. Chomsky himself rarely made any effort to provide empirical evidence for his theories, although other people, of course, have.

(Costall, 2007). So instead of stimulus-response we had stimulus-cognition-response, but the basics of the analysis of human behaviour was unchanged. Just like the behaviourists, cognitivists emphasised that human beings were passive beings who only reacted to stimulus, and also emphasised that, just like behaviourism, psychology was to remain the science of prediction and control.

And it was obvious why this had to be the case. Because the model here was the digital computer and of course, what is the digital computer but a stimulus-response machine? And we all know this. After all, what do our computers, laptops, mobile phones etc. do when we switch them on? The answer is, of course, that they don't do anything. They don't do anything unless we, the human operators, tell them to do something. In other words, they don't produce a response without a stimulus.

And this is not something extrinsic about digital computers: it is something intrinsic because cognitivist theories are *homuncular*. By which I mean, cognitivist theories are vulnerable to the homuncular argument.

To explain the homuncular argument think about the game of chess, or *Go*, or poker, or whatever. All these games have rules. Now, when 'one' is playing these games, who is it that uses these rules (for example, to decide whether or not a rule is legitimate or illegitimate?). The answer is simple: the players do or (if you are one of the players) you do. It's ridiculous to argue that it is *the rules themselves* that play the game. Now, to take another example. Look at a picture. Who is it that is looking at the picture? Obviously, again, you are. It is ridiculous to answer that it is the picture itself which is looking at the picture or that the picture could make judgements (aesthetic or otherwise) based on its own content. A picture remains just swiggles and colours hanging on an art gallery wall without a human being to come along and interpret it.

But now: think of the rules inside the head of a human being (conceptualised as an information processor). Who uses them? The obvious answer is that there must be some other being 'inside' the mind/brain that interprets these rules or pictures. But what 'powers' the cognition of this other being? Obviously, since we are cognitivists, we have decided that the only method of cognition is to have rules acting on representations. So, therefore, this other being (which is normally termed a 'homunculus') must have rules and representations inside *its* head. But what interprets these? The answer, again, must be that this homunculus has another homunculus inside its head, which is in turn 'powered' by ... and we are into an infinite regress. Another way this is sometimes phrased is in the context of representationalism. If one conceptualises vision as having a 'picture' inside one's head, who 'watches' this picture? Obviously a homunculus, which in turn needs another homunculus to see the vision in its head and so on. This is sometimes termed the 'Cartesian Theatre'.

Now the homunculus argument is well known in the world of philosophy of mind (see for example Maslin, 2001). But it is usually misinterpreted as being merely an interesting logical paradox: we must, we are told, 'ground the regress'. But the point is that unless we can do this, then cognitivist psychology is simply not working as a model of thought. What do we want to explain? Conscious thought. And we invoke rules and representations to do this. But the homunculus argument demonstrates that a fundamental logical error is being made here: cognitivism *presupposes what it is supposed to explain.* The (alleged) existence of rules and representations in reality explains nothing, as what has to be invoked to make the theory work (a conscious being (homunculus) that uses the rules and representations) is in reality what we wanted to understand in the first place. Cognitivist explanations for consciousness are an explanation for consciousness that begins: 'first, let's presuppose the existence of consciousness ... then ...' or (to make it clearer) like a recipe for cake that has, as one of its ingredients 'cake'.

Of course this is widely understood to be a problem even within EP, and Stephen Pinker has attempted to answer it: as well he might, because Pinker understands, as so few of his critics do, that if the Computational Theory of Mind (CTM) cannot 'deal with' the homunculus argument then it fails as a model of human cognition and that if the CTM falls, then EP could not possibly be true. His solution is worth quoting in full.

> The computational theory of mind also rehabilitates once and for all the infamous homunculus. A standard objection to the idea that thoughts are internal representations (an objection popular among scientists trying to show how tough-minded they are) is that a representation would require a little man in the head to look at it, and the little man would require an even littler man to look at the representations inside him, and so on, ad infinitum. But once more we have the spectacle of the theoretician insisting to the electrical engineer that if the engineer is correct his workstation must contain hordes of little elves. Talk of homunculi is indispensable in computer science. Data structures are read and interpreted and examined and recognized and revised all the time, and the subroutines that do so are unashamedly called 'agents,' 'demons,' 'supervisors,' 'monitors,' 'interpreters,' and 'executives' Why doesn't all this homunculus talk lead to an infinite regress? *Because an internal representation is not a lifelike photograph of the world, and the homunculus that 'looks at it' is not a miniaturized copy of the entire system, requiring its entire intelligence.* That indeed would have explained nothing. Instead, a representation is a set of symbols corresponding to aspects of the world, and each homunculus is required only to react in a few circumscribed ways to some of the symbols, a feat far simpler than what the system as a whole does. The intelligence of the system emerges from the activities of the not-so-intelligent mechanical demons inside it. The point, first made by Jerry Fodor in 1968, has been succinctly put by Daniel Dennett: (Note; the rest of this quote comes from Dennett). 'Homunculi are bogeymen only if they duplicate entire the talents they are rung in to explain. If one can get a team or committee of relatively ignorant, narrow-minded, blind homunculi to produce the intelligent behaviour of the whole, this is progress. A flow chart is typically the organizational chart of a committee of homunculi (investigators, librarians, accountants, executives); each box specifies a homunculus by

prescribing a function without saying how it is accomplished (one says, in effect: put a little man in there to do the job). If we then look closer at the individual boxes we see that the function of each is accomplished by subdividing it via another flow chart into still smaller, more stupid homunculi. Eventually this nesting of boxes within boxes lands you with homunculi so stupid (all they have to do is remember whether to say yes or no when asked) that they can be, as one says, "replaced by a machine." One discharges fancy homunculi from one's scheme by organizing armies of idiots to do the work.' (Pinker: 2003, 79)

One might note in passing that this is the only discussion of this issue in the book *How the Mind Works*. This is interesting in that it's not going too far to say that if this argument fails then the whole cognitivist (and, therefore EP) enterprise not only fails, but doesn't get off the ground in the first place. In other words, if Pinker's counter-argument fails then cognitivism (and therefore EP) *isn't even wrong*. It's not even a theory, as it presupposes what it is allegedly trying to explain. So we'll take the argument a bit more seriously than Pinker and go through it step by step. To begin at the beginning.

'Talk of homunculi is indispensable in computer science. Data structures are read and interpreted and examined and recognized and revised all the time, and the subroutines that do so are unashamedly called "agents," "demons," "supervisors," "monitors," "interpreters," and "executives." ' What Pinker is talking about here is not so much computer science *per se*, as computer programming. And it's true that on computers, which are designed by human beings, built by human beings, bought by human beings and used by human beings, computer programs are sometimes run (by human beings). And, of course these computer programs were also designed by human beings, written by human beings, written in computer languages which were designed and built by human beings, and which, finally, were 'based' on machine code, (i.e. zeros and ones), a way of programming digital computers that was thought up by human beings. It's true that human beings sometimes *choose to talk* about 'interpreters' and 'executives' etc. (it's not the case that the computers themselves chose this way of talking) because it's useful and it fits in with humans' predilection for anthropomorphising inanimate objects. We call our car 'she', Russians fight for 'the Motherland', we call the clock tower in London 'Big Ben' and so forth.

Clearly this paragraph does not dispute the homuncular argument: instead it gives weight to it. *Human beings* isolate aspects of computer code and *choose* to call them agents etc. Again, this is conscious human beings posing as the homunculus. Pinker's argument will only hold if it was the computer code *itself* which decided to term aspects of itself agents, demons and so forth. So this point is irrelevant.

We then turn to the major argument. Dennett (quoted by Pinker) argues:

'Homunculi are bogeymen only if they duplicate entire the talents they are rung in to explain.'

But this misses the point of the homuncular argument. The point is not *the amount of work* that the homunculus is supposed to do, as Dennett seems to think. The point is the *mechanism* by which the homunculus thinks. The homuncular argument questions the idea that (to quote Pinker earlier) 'thinking is computation' by which he means algorithmic computation. For the purpose of the argument the complexity of the code (i.e. the algorithmic code) or 'how many' lines of code there are is irrelevant. To see what I mean let's look at how Dennett frames the argument.

'If one can get a team or committee of relatively ignorant, narrow-minded, blind homunculi to produce the intelligent behaviour of the whole, this is progress. '

So: say we have rules implanted in the human brain: to understand whether or not a sentence is grammatical or not, say (or it could be to decide whether nor not something is a representation of something or not: it's not important. The point is that the decision making process is carried out by algorithms). And we have to have a homunculus to understand

and explain these rules. OK: so far we are in agreement. But then the problem remains: what 'powers' the cognition inside the homunculus's head? As argued above, it might have to be another homunculus, which would leave us in a situation of infinite regress. But Dennett and Pinker have another solution. Perhaps there are not one but two homunculi, but each one is half as intelligent as the first one? And then, upon being asked how these homunculi cognise we can argue that they in turn 'break down' into four homunculi (again, half as 'stupid') and so forth and etc.

Now it's obvious here that at least in the short term Dennett hasn't made his situation easier. He's made it harder. Instead of one homunculus, he now has dozens, then hundreds, then thousands, all of which, in turn have to have other homunculi behind them. And one might, as well, ask some extremely hard and sceptical questions about how this 'regress' would actually work in practice. Dennett writes:

> A flow chart is typically the organizational chart of a committee of homunculi (investigators, librarians, accountants, executives); each box specifies a homunculus by prescribing a function without saying how it is accomplished (one says, in effect: put a little man in there to do the job). If we then look closer at the individual boxes we see that the function of each is accomplished by subdividing it via another flow chart into still smaller, more stupid homunculi. (Pinker, 2003: 79)

Of course, in the managerial reality which Dennett is alluding to, again, organisation flowcharts are written, printed and interpreted by human beings: it's not a 'natural' state of affairs. Nor is it true that in an organisation, the people underneath the managers are 'stupider' than the people above, nor are their tasks less complex, in any *objective* sense (one could argue the converse, actually). It is question begging in an extreme form to argue that 'well, natural selection, in a real world situation, would work out how to create a "flowchart" and would work out which homunculi would go in which "place" and would work out the precise details of how the relationship between all these little information processors would work.' What we are trying to understand is: is this actually possible? Dennett is essentially arguing: 'well let's assume it is, and then let's go on to consider....'

Appealing to computer science won't help either, because in reality, it is human beings that make all these decisions when programming a computer. Dennett is essentially trying to lay out a design for a computer programme *that writes itself.* At the moment, there is no computer program that writes itself, nor is there any sign of any being designed anytime soon. So a little more detail on what amounts to the design of what amounts to an informational perpetual motion machine would be appreciated.

In essence, therefore, at this point in the argument we have still explained nothing. We still have the homuncular problem, and we still have the problem of how to 'ground' the regress. It is now that Dennett provides his answer (and it should be noted that he and Pinker seem to think that this one sentence suffices as the key argument for the philosophical position on which both of them have built their careers).

'Eventually this nesting of boxes within boxes lands you with homunculi so stupid (all they have to do is remember whether to say yes or no when asked) that they can be, as one says, "replaced by a machine." '(Pinker, 2003: 79).

What Dennett is alluding to here is binary machine code. Eventually we 'decompose' the homunculi until we have many, many, mega-stupid homunculi that are only capable of 'saying' zero or one. But the key point here is 'when asked.' Who is it that is doing the asking? And how do they know what answer to give? After all, they can't be flickering on and off at random. Clearly they are still capable of some form of cognition in that they must perform some kind of calculation even to provide an answer to a question ('replaced by a machine'. What kind of machine?). And if the answer is that they are performing some kind of calculation then according to cognitivism this *must* be by some kind of algorithmic process and therefore the regress is not grounded. (One might add that one cannot make inferences about the complexity of the question from the complexity of the answer. Is it true that E=mc^2 is a question that can be answered 'yes' or 'no' but that doesn't mean that no cognition is required to answer it correctly).

But in fact the situation is worse than this. Again, who is asking them the question to which the answer is 'yes' or 'no'? Other homunculi? If so, we are in a position of infinite regress. Or the homunculi 'above' them in the flowchart? But in that case, again, these 'ultra-stupid' homunculi must have access to information that the 'smarter' homunculi do not have, and so they can't be quite as stupid as they seem (at least in this sense). And this again would seem to presuppose cognition of a form, and therefore calculation and therefore more regress.

Moreover, another key point is *'remember* when to say yes or no when asked'. What does this mean? That they store information and respond to requests to provide it in binary form upon a formal request? But this again implies algorithmic calculation and again the regress is not grounded.

Finally, Dennett clearly means to remind us of the fact that computer programs are ultimately made up of binary computer code. But in reality binary code is not made up of stupid homunculi that could be 'replaced by a machine'. Binary code is programmed by human beings who choose to place zeros and ones in specific places to perform tasks that human beings want a computer to perform. And this machine code does not sit there, inert. It is information, passed from a human to a computer in a human designed programming language. So where did this program come from? Again, in reality it is programmed by a human being: and so in the cognitivist world this must be a homunculus and again the regress is not grounded

Therefore, the 'dissolution' or 'pyramid of morons' homuncular argument won't work either.

Therefore the cognitivist model simply won't work as a model of human cognition.

Information Processing

What else is there? There is also the information processing view of cognition. To quote Pinker again:

> The computational theory of mind has quietly entrenched itself in neuroscience, the study of the physiology of the brain and nervous system. *No corner of the field is untouched by the idea that information processing is the fundamental activity of the brain.* Information processing is what makes neuroscientists more interested in neurons than in glial cells, even though the glia take up more room in the brain. The axon (the long output fibre) of a neuron is designed, down to the molecule, to propagate information with high fidelity across long separations, and when its electrical signal is transduced to a chemical one at the synapse (the junction between neurons), the physical format of the information changes while the information itself remains the same. And as we shall see, the tree of dendrites (input fibres) on each neuron appears to perform the basic *logical and statistical* operations underlying computation. (Pinker, 2003: 83).

To admit one point first: it is true that, possibly under the influence of cognitivism, neuroscience used to pay insufficient evidence to glial (and other) cells. However, it is now realised that this was a mistake: in certain areas of the brain (for example the cerebellum) there are far more glial cells than neurons (as Pinker points out). However, as Pinker *fails* to point out, glial cells are absolutely crucial in terms of synapse development and other essential neurological phenomena: the old fashioned, cognitivist influenced way of discussing glia as if their only purpose was to 'support' neurons is unfortunately still extant, but such language is far less prevalent than it used to be. ('Virtually every aspect of brain development and function involves a neuron-glial partnership. Therefore, the answer to every important question about brain disease will also involve glia.')((Barres, 2008: 437). However, even given Pinker's old-fashioned over-emphasis on neurons most neuroscience is simply not that influenced by the 'information processing' view of the brain, as a quick look through the relevant literature will demonstrate (there is no mystery why: much of neuroscience is aimed towards specific medical research programmes, e.g. Alzheimer's disease, and the language of cognitivism is of little use in these discussions). Even when it is, the specific way in which neuroscientists talk about information processing does not support the thrust of Pinker's argument as we will see. But more of that later.

However in any case, even if one was to grant all of Pinker's point, it would still be irrelevant. So what if a lot of people think something is the case?[3] This is simply the argument from authority. The key point is: do logical arguments support Pinker's position?

So: do they? We have seen that Pinker's arguments against the homuncular argument do not hold up. But there is another argument against cognitivism, the so-called 'Chinese Room' argument. Do Pinker's arguments hold up against this thought experiment?

The Chinese Room Argument

The philosopher John Searle's Chinese room argument has been expressed in many ways. However, what I want to discuss here is the extent to which Searle's argument is really a restatement of the homuncular argument above. Searle begins (in his initial paper, Searle, 1980) by positing a man in a sealed room. He has a book of instructions (this book, importantly, is in the form of rules). There is one entrance/exit to the room, and through this people pass him Chinese symbols, which he can then look up in the book. When he looks up a symbol the

---

3 And indeed Pinker would be the first to agree with this if it was pointed out, correctly, that cognitivist arguments are less and less fashionable in psychology proper.

book 'gives him an order' (in the form of a rule/algorithm), and he then goes to the 'database' of Chinese symbols which has also been provided for him in the room (for the purposes of the thought experiment this is taken to be exhaustive). He then gets the 'appropriate' symbol and sticks it in the 'exit' hole (Searle, 1980).

The point of Searle's experiment is that whereas, from the 'outside' it might seem that there is a native Chinese speaker inside the room, 'we' see that in fact no such being exists. The person inside the room has competence, but no understanding, because s/he does not *understand* the *meaning* of any of the symbols. S/he is simply manipulating symbols.

The discussion of meaning here should remind us of the discussion of Shannon's concept of 'information' above and in fact it is the same point that is being made. Actually in a more formal statement of the same argument he made later on, Searle made this point explicit: programs are to do with 'syntax' (i.e. a formal command or set of commands that organise symbols) whereas human beings deal with semantics i.e. meaning.

The point I want to stress here is that this is really the homuncular argument in a different setting. Here the man/woman inside the Chinese room is the homunculus. It is the man/woman who provides the 'spark': who picks up the symbols, who looks up the 'meaning' (more of this later) of them in the book, who picks up the symbols and feeds them back to the outside world again. So, the first point of Searle's argument is that the rules themselves don't do anything: the whole system needs a homunculus to 'get it going' (it's noticeable that almost everyone, hardline cognitivists included, accept this basic point).

But Searle's argument is a homunculus without the infinite regress. And in reality of course (OF COURSE!) without the infinite regress the whole argument grinds to a halt. Because obviously (OBVIOUSLY!) the Chinese Room couldn't work, and it couldn't work because syntax *is not* in fact separable from semantics. To see why this is an important point, we have to return to the work of Noam Chomsky.

The key point of Chomsky's Colourless Green Ideas Sleep Furiously sentence, and one of the key points of Searle's Chinese Room argument is to separate out 'syntax' from 'semantics', syntax being to do with the grammatical 'form' of a sentence and semantics to do with its meaning. And the reason that this was important was that if you want to 'mathematicise' so to speak, linguistics (and then cognition) then concentrating on the logical, structural form of language made this task a lot easier. It also made it a lot more 'objective' (what else?). After all, whether a word is a noun, or a verb, is an objective fact. What a word *means* is much more subjective (especially if you then go on to ask what the word means *to you*). So this was a fairly crucial distinction.

And it is also the distinction Searle is getting at. What Searle is trying to show is that syntactic form is *a necessary but not sufficient* pre-requisite for semantics. In the room, after all, the person can grasp the form (which is given to him in the form of rules) of the sentences, he understands, presumably, the structural relations between the symbols given to him, but he doesn't have a clue what any of the symbols actually *mean*.

Likewise, in Chomsky's argument, the *form* of the sentence is Adj-Adj-Noun-Verb-Adverb (Colourless Green Ideas Sleep Furiously). We recognise this as a sentence (that is as a grammatical sentence) even though it has no meaning. It has syntax, but no semantic content. (Chomsky, 1957: 15).

It's worthwhile looking at that sentence for a bit longer, because, again, although this is an absolutely crucial argument for the cognitivist enterprise it tends to be 'zoomed past' at a very great speed. To begin with, what seems like a trivial point: the sentence is not quite as meaningless as it was when Chomsky wrote it as: meanings change over time and words take on new meanings. *Ipso facto*, sentences that were perfectly meaningful to people in the past now mean nothing. One need only go back a few hundred years and most of us find ourselves straining over some of the denser passages of Shakespeare. Go back a few hundred more and large chunks of Chaucer or Langland are now completely incomprehensible to most normal English speakers. And yet these sentences are perfectly grammatical. But they prove, not Chomsky's point, but instead the simple fact that words change meaning over time. Likewise, one can imagine a time in a few hundred years time when Chomsky's sentence WILL be meaningful: perhaps the word 'sleep' will take on more meanings, or perhaps 'furiously' will. It's significant here that, to repeat, Chomsky's sentence is less meaningless than it was because the word 'green' has now taken on a new meaning. 'Green ideas' used to mean nothing, but now, of course, green means 'ecological' as well as the colour. And of course colourless can mean 'insipid' as well as 'without colour'. So already the first three words of the sentence, which used to be absolutely and completely meaningless, can now mean 'insipid ecological ideas', which is of course, perfectly meaningful.

Secondly there is the element of context, which helps give us meaning. You can take any English sentence, which is both meaningful and grammatical, and rip some of the words out of context to make it seem meaningless. For example, take a headline on today's Wikinews.

'NASA launches space shuttle Atlantis on STS–125, the fifth and final service mission to the Hubble Space Telescope'.

It's very obviously in context what STS–125 means, but remove that context and the word suddenly becomes meaningless, as does the part of the sentence.

'Atlantis on STS–125 the fifth'.

Suddenly these words are meaningless but this is only because we have omitted a comma and surrounding words. Add in these and the phrase becomes completely meaningful again.

In the same way, look at the Chomsky sentence above, and add in some punctuation marks and some surrounding text.

'The senators, dreaming of colourless green ideas, sleep, furiously kicking the covers about on their hotel beds'

Not exactly the most common of English sentences, but nonetheless perfectly meaningful as long as we interpret 'green' to mean 'ecological' and 'colourless' to mean 'insipid'.

But the most profound problem here is that Chomsky is

committing himself to the idea that any sentence with the grammatical form described above will be recognised as being grammatical, regardless of meaning. But words don't 'have' grammatical form. Instead human beings choose to use them in certain ways which are then interpreted *post hoc* as being grammatical. For example, take a common or garden English word like shop window. A noun, obviously, but I have recently seen it used as a verb 'to shop window', meaning to show off a product. Google is an even more obvious example: once a rarely used word for a particularly high number used in maths, now an all-purpose verb ('Just Google XXXX and ...') And in fact all words are like this. For example, a quick Google search on this very topic quickly shows that in management/IT 'architect' is well on the way to being used as a verb (to architect a program now means to look at the technical architecture on which it will run, apparently).

So let's see if Chomsky's theory holds up: is it true that we will see every sentence with the syntactic form Adj-Adj-Noun-Verb-Adverb, and recognise it as being grammatical even if it is meaningless? Remember, the following sentence has exactly the same form (and some of the same words) as 'Colourless Green Ideas Sleep Furiously'.

'Arboreal Mammary Media Paragraph Well'. (Note: To 'paragraph' means 'to divide into paragraphs').

This is just gibberish, and yet according to Chomsky and Pinker we should 'all' immediately identify this as being grammatical, though it has no meaning.

In other words, in practice, syntax cannot be separated from meaning, because in reality words 'are' not nouns or verbs or whatever. Instead human beings *classify* words and *use* words as verbs, nouns, adverbs and so on.

The Chinese Room again

So in reality it's not at all clear that the Chinese Room would actually work, because it's not at all clear what classification system could be created such that words, let alone sentences, could be classified without reference to meaning. Nor is it clear how words or sentences could be classified without reference to background knowledge (which helps us understand meaning) or creativity (again, hard to explain in a purely rule bound, deterministic format). Finally it is not at all clear how a purely rule bound system could function in what is (again, Searle doesn't point this out but it's obvious from context) a stimulus-response format. It would be interesting to set up an experiment to see whether or not the Chinese Room, or anything remotely resembling it, could function in a real world context or even if it could, if it could function in 'real-time'.

In any case, Searle's point is that even if you could create a system that treats language purely as a formal, syntactic system (and my argument above is that you can't) that would be necessary but not sufficient for creating a semantic system: i.e. a system that grasps meaning. For EP to be correct, this argument would have to be refuted.

Pinker's Retort

Here is Pinker's argument as to why the Chinese Room argument won't work.

'Searle's tactic is to appeal over and over to our common sense. You can almost hear him saying, "Aw, c'mon! You mean to claim that the guy understands Chinese?'?!!! Geddadahere! He doesn't understand a word!! He's lived in Brooklyn all his life!!" and so on. But the history of science has not been kind to the simple intuitions of common sense, to put it mildly. ' (Pinker, 2003: 94).

This is interesting in that it at least acknowledges that to the 'man in the street' it is *not* common sense that the brain is a digital computer, and that such a claim is profoundly counter-intuitive. And he argues that just because something is not common-sensical that does not mean we should not accept it. That is true. But it is also true that much pseudo-science is also not commonsensical (homeopathy for example). So this isn't so much an argument as a pre-argument, a claim that cognitivism/EP should be considered as a serious theory. But it is not any evidence that it is therefore true.

Pinker goes on:

> My own view is that Searle is merely exploring facts about the English word understand. People are reluctant to use the word unless certain stereotypical conditions apply: the rules of the language are used rapidly and unconsciously, and the content of the language is connected to the beliefs of the whole person. If people balk at using the vernacular word understand to embrace exotic conditions that violate the stereotype but preserve the essence of the phenomenon, then nothing, scientifically speaking, is really at stake. We can look for another word, or agree to use the old one in a technical sense; who cares? The explanation of what makes understanding work is the same. Science, after all, is about the principles that make things work, not which things are 'really' examples of a familiar word. If a scientist explains the functioning of the human elbow by saying it is a second-class lever, it is no refutation to describe a guy holding a second-class lever made of steel and proclaim, 'But look, the guy doesn't have three elbows!' (Pinker, 2003: 95).

This is a fairly complex passage, but reading it closely reveals it to be yet another exercise in question begging. The key sentence, I think is 'Science, after all, is about the principles that make things work …'. This is true. But this begs the question: *is it in fact the case that the brain works by algorithms working on representations*? If this was the case, the Pinker would have won the argument and I wouldn't be sitting here writing this book. Yet again, Pinker is merely clearing the ground for an argument: he is making it clear that this theory is possible and should be taken seriously. And we sit and wait for the argument itself. But the argument never comes. And finally Pinker points out that the idea that thought arises, so to speak, from meat, is equally incredible, which is true but irrelevant because we know for a fact that human beings are conscious, whereas whether or not computers could ever be conscious is precisely what is in question.

Round Three

In *How the Mind Works* he then goes on to discuss the theories
of Roger Penrose (we met Penrose before, in the context of
his discussions with Stephen Hawking), in his book *The
Emperor's New Mind*. (Penrose, 1990). However, he limits his
discussion entirely to Penrose's own theories (Penrose has
attempted to link quantum mechanics to consciousness). I
am in sympathy with this critique as I don't buy Penrose's
ideas either. However, this misses the key point, yet again:
just because Penrose is wrong it does not follow that Pinker
(or anyone else in the field of EP) is right. Indeed, looking
through *The Emperor's New Mind* there are many interesting
snippets that one might have thought would be greatly of
interest to anyone in the cognitivist/EP camp. For example,
after acknowledging that on a *cursory, superficial* glance, the
actions of neurons might seem similar to those of logic gates
in a digital computer Penrose continues ...

> we should (also) consider various *differences* between brain
> action and present-day computer action that might possibly be
> of significance. In the first place I have oversimplified somewhat
> in my description of the firing of a neuron as an all-or-nothing
> phenomenon. That refers to a single pulse travelling along the
> axon, but in fact when a neuron 'fires' it emit's a whole sequence
> of such pulses in quick succession. Even when a neuron is not
> activated, it emits pulses, but only at a slow rate. When it fires,
> it is the frequency of these successive pulses which increases
> enormously. There is also a probabilistic aspect of neuron firing.
> The same stimulus does not always produce the same result.
>
> Moreover, brain action does not have quite the exact timing
> that is needed for electronic computer currents; and it should
> be pointed out that the action of neurons at a maximum rate
> of about 1000 times per second is very much slower than that
> of the fastest electronic circuits, by a factor of about 10^{-6}. Also,
> unlike the very precise wiring of an electronic computer,
> there would appear to be a good deal of randomness and
> redundancy ... (in the brain) ... there are other factors in the
> brain's favour. With logic gates there are only very few input

and output wires (say three or four at most), whereas neurons may have huge numbers of synapses on them. (For an extreme example, those neurons of the cerebellum known as Purkinje cells have about 80000 excitatory synaptic endings). Also, the total number of neurons in the brain is still in excess of the number of transistors in even the largest computer: probably 10 to the power of 11 for the brain and 'only' about 10 to the power of 9 for the computer!' (Penrose, 1990: 510).

Penrose then goes on to discuss the fascinating phenomenon of neuro-plasticity which will be discussed later on (and the even more fascinating topic of neuro-genesis): brain features which do not seem to have any analogue in the behaviour of digital computers.

Obviously these arguments can be argued against: but the key point is that despite surface appearances, a closer look reveals that in many key respects the brain would seem to be *quite unlike* a digital computer. What does Pinker, or, for that matter, the majority of people working in EP think about this? The answer is, we do not know. Overwhelmingly it is simply *assumed* that the brain is a digital computer and the discussion moves onwards on the grounds set by that assumption. And we see again why the cognitivists were so keen not to have their new 'science' be reducible to neuroscience: there was always, one suspects, the vague fear that when neuroscientists started to make real discoveries, the cognitivists wouldn't like what was discovered. And so it proved.

Is the Mind Modular?

So, to conclude, we have seen that the evidence that the brain is an information processing device, similar to a digital computer (at least in abstract description, i.e. as a Turing Machine) is poor. It has little empirical data to support it, and the logical arguments to support it are either false or do not make sense. Moreover, as we shall see in the next chapter, more and more cognitive scientists are now abandoning the idea (description of these new ideas will also involve the discussion of even more data showing that the information processing view of cognition is false).

But what about the idea that the brain is modular? This is even more important for EP. Indeed, unless the brain is modular, and not just modular but massively modular, then EP simply cannot be framed as a coherent theory. EP needs modularity to demonstrate that these modules evolved for the pre-historic African Savannah. This is, as we have seen, what EP is all about.

Now, the idea that the mind/brain is modular derives from the cognitivism's earliest assumptions. To repeat: Newtonian-type science is reductionist (i.e. it posits the idea that things must be cut into smaller and smaller pieces); but it is also Platonic, at least in a mathematical sense.[4] For example, take atoms. In Newton's time (and this is made even clearer if we look at the Ancient Greek views of atoms) one (theoretically speaking)' cut things' into smaller and smaller pieces, until we got little 'blocks' of matter, which were indivisible: atoms.

Now the reason this was done was because it made the sums easier to do. If one assumes that everything is essentially the same (that is, the context doesn't really matter), then it's much easier to formulate causal, deterministic laws that have universal application: and, after Newton, physicists assumed that this was their job. Small, shiny, *identical* atoms were therefore presumed to 'make up' the world of matter. Obviously, in the real world this wasn't the case, so the laws of physics don't 'really' apply to real objects: they apply to mathematised idealisations of reality. In the 'real world' the laws of physics only work *ceteris paribus*. (Cartwright, 1999)

So cognitivists were looking for internal discrete geo-metrical 'shapes' or 'forms' that could be seen to exist in a deterministic causal chain (i.e. causal in relation to behaviours): in other words, atom like things. And mental

---

4   This explains why the cognitivists were reductionist and anti-reductionist at the same time. Yes they wanted to 'reduce' things, but to the aetherial world of 'information', NOT to brain states.

modules fitted this description down to a T. The problem for the cognitivists was that the 'chain' of causation which led from mental module (consisting of information processing/ rules and representations apparatus) to behaviour 'started' at the mental module. This begged the question: where did the 'mental model' come from? What 'caused' it?

The EPers thought they had the answer to this, which would then 'tie in' psychology to a real science: the 'modern synthesis' of neo-Darwinism, which by the mid 1980s was extremely well established. *Natural Selection,* in this view, led to the development of mental modules, which then led to behaviour. A causal chain was therefore created, going back to natural selection, which in turn, of course, was compatible with the basic laws of physics. So the causal chain went: natural selection, selected the appropriate mental models (adapted to Neolithic Africa) which then led to human behaviour. And with natural selection ultimately reducible to physics, finally, therefore, psychology could take its place as a proper science: i.e. a reductionist, deterministic, mathematical, quantitative science of predictive laws.

But of course, in order to make this view of psychology work, the mind has to be modular. So: is, in fact, the mind modular?

To begin with it's worth stressing that the idea that the mind is modular in some sense has a good deal more evidence for it than many other aspects of the EP thesis, given that it is based on reasonably rigorous levels of argumentation taken from linguistics and philosophy. However a number of points should be explained first.

The key and best argument for the idea that the brain is, to a certain extent, modular is taken from the theorising of Noam Chomsky, who provided evidence for a Language Acquiring Module. However, as Buller (2005) points out just because there is one module in the human brain it does not, therefore, follow that there are many (or for that matter more than one). Indeed, one could argue the contrary. Perhaps the language 'instinct' is so strange and unique that it is only in the field of language that natural selection facilitated the creation of such a cognitive feature. So even if the evidence for a LAM was watertight, it would not necessarily prove the existence of the other modules that, to stress the point, EP *needs* to function as a worthwhile scientific theory.

The second point is less often made but just as important: even if the mind/brain is to a certain extent modular, it also does not follow that it is *massively* modular in the way needed by EP. This is a point that has been made, tirelessly, by none other than Jerry Fodor himself. Fodor, in the *Modularity of Mind* proposed a number of cognitive modules, yes, but only for so-called 'lower' intellectual functions. He did not think that modularity could ever function as a meaningful explanation for 'conscious' 'higher level' intellectual thought processes, which is, let's face it, what we are all really interested in. The reason why is quite simple: it's to do with 'triggering'. Let's take the example of a real (proposed) module: one for human face recognition.

Imagine you have three modules in your brain, one to do with human face recognition, one to do with animal face recognition, and one to do with everything else. So in other words, if we saw a human face module A would be triggered, if we saw an animal's face module B would be triggered and if we saw anything else then module C would be triggered. These modules would be in the form of an Evolved Psychological Mechanism (EPM) as proposed by Buss (1994).

The key point is the mechanism of 'entry' to the information processing system (i.e. the brain). A 'piece' or 'bit' of information enters the brain. Now, how do we know what module it should be assigned to? Obviously we need another module that has to make this decision. So it needs to know, essentially, what is the difference between a human face, a dog face, and everything else. But of course that information is supposed to have been decided by the modules themselves. So this 'meta-module' would have to know everything that was contained within the basic modules themselves. So why bother having the modules in the first place? This would seem to be an insoluble problem.[5]

Fodors uses this argument to stress that he always thought that modules could *only* work for low level, almost 'pre-cognitive' phenomena where the 'triggering' of the modules would be more or less automatic. And in *The Mind Doesn't Work That Way* he stresses something that is surely true: the fantasies of cognitivism notwithstanding, we really have no idea whatsoever of how the mass of the brain works, nor are we really any further forward in understanding it than we were forty years ago (if one assumes, as I do, that cognitivism has been a huge 'red herring' in psychology, one might argue that we actually know less than we did forty years ago, in that we now 'know' lots of things that aren't true).

So, to repeat, EP doesn't just have to prove that there is a Language Acquiring Device, although it does. And it doesn't even have to prove that there are 'low level' cognitive modules as well, although it has to do that too. To make sense, EP has to prove that there are higher level cognitive modules too, and lots of them. So, let's look at the evidence.

Let's begin by discussing Chomsky's Language Acquiring Module. There is, unfortunately, no space to discuss Chomsky's theories in full here. However a number of points need to be made before we continue. Remember, the evidence for Chomsky's LAM is by far the best for any form of module.

---

5 Except of course that some scholars in the EP tradition think they have solved it. Barret, for example, argues that the problem can be solved by comparison with the way that allegedly similar problems are solved in biochemistry. But of course, despite Barret's hopeful use of the word 'information' throughout a description of this process, human biochemistry is perfectly describable in terms of...well...biochemistry. The use of the language of information processing is not necessary. It is not enough to state that the modularity problem can be solved. Obviously it can. The issue is: can it be solved by a modular *information processing* system? And here the failure of GOFAI, and failure of cognitivists to solve the frame problem tells its own story, because, given that this 'modularity' problem can be restated as a problem of how an information processing device can decide what information is relevant, it can be seen that this is really the frame problem in another guise (Barret and Kurzban, 2006).

Chomsky

It's with a sense of relief that one moves from the work of Buss, Pinker *et al.* to looking at Chomsky's work, as at least Chomsky has discussed his work in detail and has engaged in debate with his intellectual opponents. As mentioned earlier, the primary scholars of EP tend to ignore any opposition and simply assume that anyone who opposes EP is anti-science or anti-evolution.

But nonetheless, and despite that fact that Chomsky remains one of the most significant intellects of the 20th century, it's only fair to point out that for most linguists, serious doubts still remain over the truth (or otherwise) of Chomsky's main theories. What Chomsky did was to reorientate the direction of linguistics from a mainly descriptive, taxonomic science, to one that was more concerned with explanations, and causal relations. He also greatly stressed the importance of creativity in language use (behaviourist approaches to language tended to downplay this) and also highlighted certain theoretical problems with behaviourist approaches to, for example, language learning. This was all to the good.

However, it's one thing to say that Chomsky has raised important research questions. It's quite another to state that his own answers to these questions are the correct ones. To repeat, it's not the task of this book to engage in an in-depth discussion of the truth or falsehood of Chomsky's theories, but it is important to point out that just because Chomsky has stated something to be the case, it does not prove it to be the case, and that the evidence for a Language Acquiring Module, is not, perhaps, as good as it ought to be. And, to repeat again: the evidence for an LAM is, by quite a good way, better than the evidence for any of the other alleged modules inside the human brain/mind.

The Language Instinct

What we are concerned with, as ever, is not Chomsky's work *per se*, but Chomsky as seen by Pinker: Pinker being the cognitive scientist who has most strongly pushed the 'Chomskyan line'. Pinker, in his works on linguistics, tends to assume that Chomsky's theories have been proven beyond all reasonable doubt. And of course there is a lot of evidence that seems to support Chomsky's theories.

And yet ... and yet ... One is continually struck, not by the fact that there is evidence that Chomsky is right, but by the fact that this evidence is not, perhaps, quite as good as it should be after more than fifty years of research. Again, it is often assumed outside linguistics that the Chomskyan approach is the bedrock of modern linguistics. But there are extremely large 'areas' of linguistics (socio-linguistics, cognitive linguistics) that owe little or nothing to the Chomskyan approach: Chomsky does *not* stand in the same relation to modern linguistics as, say, Newton does to modern physics or Galileo to modern astronomy.

And it's still startling, after more than fifty years of research in the Chomskyan tradition to see Pinker admit: 'No one has yet located a language organ or grammar gene....' (Pinker, 1994: 46). One could argue that this is because neuroscience is a 'new' science, but the 'backwardness' of neuroscience in comparison with other sciences is something of a myth. The world's oldest surgical document (and second oldest scientific document) is the Edwin Smith Papyrus which dates from the 17th century BC which talks about the brain in some detail (David, 2000). More work was done by the Greeks and scientists in the Islamic tradition. Nowadays, of course, state of the art technology can be used to look at the brain in astonishing detail, and yet we still have not found a single one of the alleged 'modules' on which EP bases its claims: not even the Language Acquiring Module, for which the evidence is strongest (See for example, Dobbs, 2005). Perhaps, therefore, we should take a closer look at Chomsky's theories.

Modularity and Language

The 'superstructure' of Chomskyan linguistics is based on

two major claims, both of which sound extremely plausible...
at first glance. The first claim is that the speed with which
human infants learn language demonstrates that they could
not possibly be being 'taught' it in any meaningful sense.
Instead, there must be some kind of 'internal' drive which
helps them to speak: or as Chomsky puts it, language is not
taught, it 'grows in the mind'. The second claim is that due
to the similarities between human languages, there must be,
in some shape or form, some kind of inbuilt constraint on the
kinds of languages that we can learn such that some linguistic
forms are simply impossible for us to learn: in other words
there must be some kind of a Universal Grammar (Chomsky
doesn't tend to use this phrase any more but that's not really
important for our argument here) to which all languages
conform.

Now, both these claims sound extremely plausible in the
abstract. It's only when we get down to the nitty-gritty that
the problems start.

To take the second (and in my opinion, weaker) claim first.
It's true that, from a certain way of looking at things, all the
world's languages have similarities. But some linguists (by no
means all) hypothesise that language only evolved once, and
that all current languages evolved from this 'ur-language'
that presumably arose in Africa, perhaps around 20,000BC or
more. If this was the case (and it's only fair to point out that
it's a highly controversial theory) then *of course* all the world's
languages would resemble each other (Greenberg, 2000).

But even if this is denied (and it's only fair to add that most
modern linguists *would* deny it), we still have to be careful
about how strong Chomsky's (and Pinker's) argument is
here. 'All' really does mean 'all' in this context. If only one
language was discovered that did not meet the strictures of
the UG (or whatever phrase is being currently used) then the
theory would be falsified. And yet at the time of writing only
a tiny minority of the world's languages (and that's the ones
that currently exist: obviously there are many others now lost
which can *never* be studied) have been looked at by Chomskyan
linguists: so how can we really know that all languages really

do have shared features? And this doesn't even get into the problem of what we mean by 'shared' features. After all we are all human, which means we are all bipeds who need to eat, breath oxygen, and drink, we all live on the same planet, we are all land animals (not birds or fish) etc. It's not that surprising that we have things in common: in other words, how do we differentiate trivial similarities between languages (which arose by chance or for trivial environmental reasons) from the significant similarities that would indicate the truth of Chomskyan theories?

This argument has not been made any easier to answer given Chomsky's vague description of what these alleged common features of language actually are. For example, one of Chomsky's claims is that truly 'human' languages, so to speak, are marked by the use of 'recursion' (which means sentences imbedded within other sentences). The problem is that if this is truly a feature of the brain then in theory human beings would be able to imbed sentences inside other sentences more or less indefinitely. But in reality, few people can understand sentences that contain more than a few recursive devices. Scholars in the Chomskyan tradition tend to attribute this problem to limits on working memory (an alleged 'short term memory' store that cognitivists claim exists in the human mind/brain) but apart from the fact that this argument depends on the existence of working memory (again, a by no means uncontroversial view) it would also seem to make the Chomskyan theory unfalsifiable in Karl Popper's sense.

Or perhaps not. Either one accepts that Chomskyan linguistics really is a kind of philosophy and is more or less unfalsifiable, or else one treats it as a scientific theory and one goes about trying to falsify it. Therefore one can infer predictive components of Chomskyan theories: for example that according to Chomsky all human (and only human) languages must contain recursion, or will conform to the UG (or whatever).[6]

---

6 It's worth pointing out that it's by no means clear that Chomsky would agree with this process. Pinker *et al.* have picked up on Chomsky's dis-

But two recent papers have challenged this ('scientific') interpretation of Chomsky's linguistics. First there is the discovery by Gentner *et al.* (2006) that starlings, too, can identify recursion: an allegedly 'human only' trait. Even more serious for Chomskyan linguistics is the discovery of the Pirahã tribe in the Amazon, and the description of their language by Daniel Everett. This is significant, because Everett argues that the Pirahã language contains no recursion, and is, therefore, 'impossible' in the Chomskyan scheme of things: that is, it does not share a feature of language that Chomsky claims to be universal. (Everett 2005) To be fair, other linguists have disagreed with Everett (cf. for example Nevins *et al.*, 2009), but this merely emphasises the fact that Chomskyan linguistics is still very much a hot and controversial topic in linguistics: it is by no means as universally accepted as Pinker implies. However, make no mistake: if Everett's view of the Pirahã was found to be accurate, this would pose extremely serious problems for this particular aspect of the Chomskyan project, which merely makes crystal clear that the jury is still out on fundamental (not trivial) aspects of Chomskyan linguistics.

The second (and in my view stronger) major argument in favour of Chomsky's theories is that of the Poverty of the Stimulus. This is the idea that children pick up language 'unfeasibly' quickly, and that they 'could not' possibly have been taught (especially the grammar) of their native languages. Therefore this is strong evidence for the idea that there must be some kind of language instinct or impulse or module that we are born with, which helps us to learn the rudiments of language.

---

like of the Empirical tradition (what Pinker derisively terms the 'Blank Slate' theory of cognition) but Chomsky's hatred of empiricism is really quite extreme: Chomsky sometimes hints that his theories are logically true, deduced like Euclid's geometry from first principles, and therefore true by definition, that he is not particularly interested in empirical proof or disproof. For the purposes of this book I am ignoring this attitude: I am in favour of the scientific method and believe that scientific theories must ultimately make 'real world' empirical predictions.

Again like many of Chomsky's arguments at first glance this sounds plausible, and, unlike many of Chomsky's arguments, it sounds plausible at second glance too. But even here there are problems, and they depend on what one means by words like 'feasibly' and 'could not'. After all, what does one mean by 'feasibly' in this context? The prediction that children pick up language quicker than we would expect is more or less meaningless unless one makes clear how quickly we would expect them to learn language in the *absence* of a language acquiring module. The philosopher Hilary Putnam, for example points out that 'it would take the average adult about four years, or 600 hours of instruction and reading to gain performance in a new language' (Putnam, 1975: 141). A child, however, encounters its native language even more frequently; 600 hours of direct-method language listening could pass in less than one year. Yet after four years of learning, the child has a small vocabulary compared to any mature student, and the child's grammatical mistakes are still numerous.' (Walker, 1999) Moreover, children have incredibly powerful motivation (unless they can talk they won't be able to ask for anything) and moreover don't have much else to do. Most of us who attempt to learn a second language in later life find it difficult, not just because we are insufficiently motivated but because we find it hard to find the time to do it. And yet after four years it is entirely possible that we would be better at speaking even a *second* language then a child is at speaking a first.

However, Chomsky would argue that this is not a fair comparison because the key point is this: adults are 'taught' a second language whereas children are not. Or, to be more precise, that the amount of information and the form of information that children are exposed to cannot possibly explain the ease and facility with which children use language. But again this is a debatable point. Scientists in the connectionist tradition (who we will encounter in the next chapter) argue that humans can infer language norms and 'rules' from the amount of language they are exposed to in 'normal life', and that they do not need formal tuition. Other scholars and scientists argue that children *are* in fact taught language, in that parents attempt to correct grammar, teach their children new words, encourage their children to talk and to read, and tell the child that certain grammatical forms are wrong. (Solan *et al.*, 2005).

This debate continues and will doubtless continue for many years to come. But, the point being made here is that, as Daniel Dennett has put it, the 'jury is still out' on the truth or otherwise of Chomskyan linguistics (Dennett, 1999). And we must remember that the evidence for a language acquiring module is ambiguous and debatable, and yet it is by far the best evidence for any kind of module in the brain.

Apart from language, the next best evidence for some kind of modularity in the mind/brain is for the modularity in the visual system.

Ecological Psychology

This is a particularly interesting field, as it brings us to a discussion of Ecological Psychology, a field created by the American psychologist J.J. Gibson. Gibson is rarely discussed by Pinker *et al*, although Fodor once attempted to debunk his work (Fodor and Pylyshyn, 1981). This is a pity as Gibson is generally agreed to be the premier experimental psychologist of the 20th century in the field of vision. And it is particularly interesting in that Gibson's work is wholly incompatible with the view of vision proposed by David Marr which as we have seen, is the bedrock for the cognitivist view of vision, and, therefore, the view of the human visual perception system as being an information processing module.

As discussed earlier, it is Noam Chomsky's language acquiring module for which the best evidence exists: Marr's vision processing module is the second best established. There is less evidence for other modules, and the evidence for the 'higher level' modules necessary for the massive modularity thesis (on which EP depends) is weaker still.

However, let's look at Marr's work at present. Marr argued that vision was computational, modular and, so to speak, mathematisable: that is, that it could be described via equations (Boden, 2006). Needless to say, these equations would function as de facto laws: again we see the quest for Newtonian certainty. And of course Marr saw the key strength of his theory, even if it proved to be wrong, was the fact that at least it was a theory, and not 'merely' empirical evidence more or less randomly 'brought together' so to speak, with no overarching hypothesis. By which he meant that he thought he had created mathematical laws of vision that gave serious, falsifiable, predictions (Marr, 1982).

In this, his main opponent was J.J. Gibson. Gibson obviously had empirical data that he alleged demonstrated the falsity of Marr's theories (or rather his disciples did: by 1982 tragically, both Marr and Gibson were dead). But his main objection was much more fundamental. Marr assumed that the basic task of vision was computational: to turn 2-D images (on the retina) into 3-D images that were 'seen' in (or by) the brain. And of course, a computer could do that. But for Gibson, more biologically minded, the purpose of vision was to facilitate an animal in doing something: finding a mate, avoiding a predator, searching for food.

Even more radically, Gibsonians denied that the visual system was about representation at all. Instead Gibsonians argued for a view they termed 'direct perception', which is the view that we *directly* perceive the environment. This is of course opposed to the 'classic' cognitivist view that perception is 'indirect': that what we perceive is not 'the world' but an internal representation of the world. Gibson argued that we do not have to 'internally represent' the world because we already have a representation of the world already: literally in front of our noses. It is called … the world.

So, what's the evidence for the Gibsonian view?

Remember what Gibson was arguing against is the idea that vision consists of an internal representation of external 'reality'. Instead we are looking for evidence that vision is a form of acting in the world, a way of *doing something.* The evidence here has been neatly summarised by the philosopher Alva Noë, who is currently propounding a view very similar to that of Gibson. So, to begin with there is:

1. Evidence from blindness. People who have been blind since birth are unable to see: in other words, they haven't learnt to see yet. Of course it could be argued that this is because various modular brain elements have withered or atrophied. However:

2. Harder to explain is evidence from experiments by Ivo Kohler in which subjects were made to wear special distorting glasses (for example, which made everything look 'upside down'). So the information coming 'into' the subject's eyes was the same, but s/he lacked the practical, 'common sense' knowledge that would help him/her relate it to his/her own experience: the subject could not walk or *make sense* of the world. As Noë puts it: 'When you put on the distorting lenses, the patterns of dependence between movement and stimulation are altered. This alteration has the effect of abrogating sensor motor knowledge or skill, even though there is no change in the intrinsic character of the stimulation ... the result is not seeing *differently,* but failing to see' (Noë, 2005: 8). Moreover there is evidence that when the eyeball itself is paralysed the eye gradually loses the ability to see: in other words the eye cannot see without moving and so to speak, 'sampling' the external environment (Noë, 2005: 13). But this is exactly the opposite of what representationalism (with its idea of static internal pictures) would predict. And of course the key idea of a cognitive visual module is that it would be a representational cognitive module.

3. There is also evidence from experiments describing 'change blindness'. For example in the famous experiment 'Gorillas in our Midst' participants were shown a basketball match, and were asked to keep track of who had the ball at any one time. At one point in the video, a woman in a gorilla suit walked onto the court. A majority of the participants

did not even see the gorilla, despite the fact that it was in plain view (Simons and Chabris, 1999). But again, this is very difficult to explain with the theory that there is an internal representation of the world which the external world is 'matched against'. Surely if this was the case when there was a mismatch, this would immediately be noted?

4. Finally, there are experiments carried out by the neurophysiologist Boris Kotchoubey.

Kotchoubey has carried out numerous experiments which measure event-related potentials, especially the P3 wave, which is associated particularly with higher-level cognitive function. This was monitored while subjects were shown various visual stimuli in a laboratory, stimuli which suggested actions. Naturally, according to the cognitivists what one would expect is that if a (sufficiently interesting) visual stimulus was produced, first one would get a pause (for cognition) associated with the P3 spike, and then one would get an action. This is the essence of cognitivism: first, stimulus, then (higher level) cognition, then response. However, experiments stubbornly failed to produce this result, showing instead P3 waves coinciding *with* the required action or even coming *after* the required action.

Kotchoubey has also carried out other experiments on reaction times to stimuli of various degrees of complexity. These show that the best predictor of reaction times is not the complexity of the decision required (as one might expect from cognitivist theories and, of course, digital computers) but instead simply the raw amount of information made available. When this reaches a certain level, people simply act, regardless of the complexity of the decision. In other words, it seems that when enough information is made available such that people *can* act, they *do* act; moreover, the P3 wave amplitude remained low, suggesting again that people were not cognitively updating their internal mental model or representation but were instead reacting directly to the information in the external world environment. Finally, and most devastatingly, visual experiments have been carried out in which subjects were given a target to look for on a screen. Other dummy visual phenomena also appeared on the screen at various times. The cognitivist theory obviously *must* predict that the most processing will be associated with seeing the actual target. In other words, the participant is perpetually updating the mental model, and when there is a match between the desired information and the perceived information, presumably there will be the internal equivalent of bells and whistles going off as our internal computer registers a match, which then provokes an action. However, this was not the case. Instead, the cortical activity associated with *behaviour* was directly stimulated, but the higher level features (i.e., those associated with cognition) dropped off (because this now indicated that the task is over, so there was no longer anything to prepare for). Again, this indicated that when information enters the brain, it stimulates action but not cognition (as that phrase is generally understood). In other words, we react *directly to* the information, not to an internal representation of the information. (See Koutchoubey 2000 and Koutcboubey 2005).

To repeat, it is very difficult to reconcile these findings with the idea that there exists an internal module for vision: it is even harder to reconcile these findings with the idea that, even if there was such a module, its 'mechanism' was that of an information processor.

Modules and Skills

The last few points above seem to be more related to issues of representation rather than modularity. But actually it's the same argument, as the key issue is: does the evidence really point to modularity? Or can the data be explained more easily in other ways?

For example, let's look at 'higher level' cognitive functions that are, allegedly, modular. Another part of brain function that is tempting to explain in modular terms is memory: this is the idea that there are short term and long term memory 'modules' from which memories are retrieve. This view is not so integral to EP as the others (it is one of the key bedrocks of cognitivism, though) so we're not going to talk about it much here: but there is one key point that must be made, and that's that, despite claims to the contrary, there is little evidence for such a static, digital computer like memory store (cf Crowder, 1982, and Shallice and Warrington, 1970). However, there *are* other experiments that, it is claimed, do show support for the modal model. However, these can usually be explained in other ways, ways that fit more closely with ecological studies of the way human beings function in their natural environments. For example, experiments have shown that it is easy for subjects, by using their fingers as *aides memoires* to improve the capacity of the short term memory stores immensely. As Glenberg has written, 'This evidence might be interpreted as evidence for a new finger Control *module* but it seems more sensible to view it as a newly acquired *skill.*'(Glenberg, 1997: 9)

This difference between a module and a skill is absolutely essential and takes us back to some crucial experiments in the 1970s which were more or less ignored at the time (to be more specific: they weren't ignored as such, but their implications were not drawn out because they were incompatible with what was, at the time, the orthodoxy). These were experiments to do with multiple skill learning. The key point here is the nature of evidence. There is, apparently, evidence for modularity. What is being asked here is: could this evidence be better reinterpreted not so much as evidence for the modularity of various cognitive functions, but as evidence that these cognitive functions are *skills* which are *learned*?

For example, in a number of experiments, the extent to which *attention* is a skill (not a module) was demonstrated. Spelke *et al.* demonstrated that, with practice, subjects could learn to read (and understand) short stories while at the same time taking dictation from spoken language. This not only demonstrated that attention was not a single-channel phenomena but also indicated that attention ...

> is based on developing and situation-specific *skills*. Particular
> examples of attentive performance should not be taken
> to reflect universal and unchanging capacities. ... Indeed
> people's abilities to develop skills in specialized situations is
> so great that it may never be possible to define general limits
> on cognitive capacity. (Spelke, Hirst, and Neisser, 1976: 229)

This was backed up by further experiments by these authors,
who provided additional evidence that automaticity
(requiring no cognitive capacity) or alternation (extremely
rapid channel switching) was not involved. In other words,
attention was a skill that could be learned, improved with
practice, and had, in theory, unlimited capacity.

Instead of being modular, Spelke *et al.* saw memory as a
kind of skill, and they compared it to the skills acquired by
athletes. In other words, the brain is not best compared to a
computer; instead, it is best conceptualized as a *muscle*. In the
same way one develops muscles via practice in the gym, the
more one practises something, the better one gets at it. One
should note that this supports the evidence from experiments
on the visual system detailed by Noë: which again proposed
that vision is something that one *does*, a skill that one learns
in the world.

High Level Modules

Finally, in 2005 we had the publication of the magisterial
Adapting Minds, by David J. Buller (Buller, 2005). I have no
intention of summarising this wonderful book here, and
merely intend to point the reader towards it. Needless to say, in
it, Buller looks through the evidence for all the various 'higher
level' modules that EP needs in order to function as a coherent
theory and finds the evidence wanting. This is devastating
for EP because, even if one accepts the cognitivist idea that
the brain is a Turing Machine (and perhaps one shouldn't)
this still doesn't mean that EP is true. The brain could still
be a *general purpose* information processor. EP really needs
the brain to be modular, and not just modular but massively

modular, or it simply fails as a serious theory. The fact that the evidence is currently so poor is not a good omen for its development as any kind of science, let alone one that will finally answer the big questions of human consciousness.

More Arguments

If this were all, it would be possible to end the book here. But actually, there still remains the question of 'What opposing model of the brain do *you* propose?' As I argued in the introduction, strictly speaking, this is irrelevant, as the burden of proof lies on the thinkers of EP. Nevertheless, we now have to raise this issue, as, according to some scholars in the EP tradition, whatever the problems with cognitivism and EP, it is 'the only game in town', as opposing theories do not, in fact, make sense. According to this view, some variety of EP is the only explanation for consciousness that is *logically possible*. Do these arguments hold up? This question will be discussed in the next chapter.

Chapter Six

EP has a fundamental 'common sense' problem, which is this. Does it not seem more likely that in the complex, ever changing environment of the primitive savannah, a brain that could evolve and adapt to complex situations would be of more value than one that had only pre-installed programs to work with? Moreover, is it not more plausible that, *ceteris paribus*, a creature that could learn from its mistakes and could therefore adapt, and prevent itself from making further mistakes (be they about mating, procuring food, avoiding accidents or whatever) would have a survival advantage over a creature that could not?

Remarkably, the answer from the EP tradition to both these questions is 'no'. Indeed, Cosmides and Tooby argue that not only is it not true that the brain is a 'general purpose' learning device, but that it is *not possible* that it should be so and that, in fact the whole concept makes no sense. Therefore, logically, the brain *must be* modular. They provide a number of statements to this effect throughout their writing and a number of versions of similar arguments to back it up. So are their arguments correct?

Cosmides and Tooby argue:

Acts are regulated by decisions, and decisions are made by procedures or decision rules. For a decision rule to produce adaptive decisions, it depends on the environment having a specific structure that corresponds to the decision rule. For a decision rule to operate, a cue must lead, with some probability, to some outcome. A decision rule that operates in all possible environments – an all-purpose inclusive fitness maximizer – would have to correspond to the structure of all possible environments. That means that no cue could be used by the general decision rule, because a cue that is associated with one outcome in one environment will be associated with another outcome in another environment. By varying the structure of the environment, any cue could become associated with any outcome with equal probability, so no cue would ever be informative. A decision rule that gains no information from the environment can produce only random decisions- which would not maximize fitness in any environment, let alone in every environment. To gain information from the environment, the procedure must already reflect some of the causal structure of the environment. Learning depends equally on cues, for discriminating success from failure and for many other subtasks as well. *The idea of an adaptation that is an all-purpose inclusive fitness maximizer is simply not coherent.* In fact, natural selection shapes decision rules and the cues they monitor. (Tooby and Cosmides, 1990: 405) (emphasis added).

Now of course the idea that acts follow from 'decision rules' (or algorithms) is the essence of cognitivism, and we have already seen why it is probably not correct: and we will look, later on in this chapter, at more up to date models of cognition that have replaced cognitivism, and are more likely to be accurate representations of how the brain actually works. So the initial premise of Cosmides and Tooby's argument is contestable. However, let's grant it for the sake of argument and look at whether or not the argument holds ups.

To begin with let's look at this sentence: 'A decision rule that operates in all possible environments – an all-purpose inclusive fitness maximizer – *would have to* correspond to the structure of *all possible environments*'. (emphasis added). Now is this in fact the case? Surely, on the contrary, a 'general purpose' algorithm does not in fact have to deal with all *possible* environments (in which case, of course it would have to be infinitely large), but merely all *existing* and *plausible* environments. For example: how would I survive if I suddenly found myself out in deep space, or in the centre of the sun or deep underwater without breathing gear? The answer is: I wouldn't. I do not in fact have 'cognitive' (or physical) apparatus that can function in *all* environments. But I do have mental and physical apparatus that would help me to survive in *most* environments that I would *plausibly* find myself in, and this is because, over time I can *learn*. Moreover, to repeat, I can't function in any given environment (without, for example, breathing apparatus and other technological aids). So it's not true that 'By varying the structure of the environment, any cue could become associated with any outcome with equal probability, so no cue would ever be informative.' It really doesn't matter whether I am a hunter-gatherer in the stone age, sitting in my office in the 21st century, or somewhere in-between, there are environmental invariants that have the same effect because I am an embodied human being: fire will always burn my bare flesh, I need oxygen to breathe, I must have adequate supplies of fluids and so on. (Why Cosmides and Tooby ignore these 'embodied' factors is an interesting question that we will look at later). The range of my possible environments are not *infinitely* variable, and therefore my brain doesn't need to be *infinitely* malleable: it just has to be malleable enough to allow me to survive. Nonetheless it will clearly be to my advantage to learn and adapt to the ever changing environment as quickly as possible. It may be that after some ecological catastrophe, the planet earth will 'die' and 'we' will all have to move off world to space stations or even to colonise a new planet. The environment in this new situation will be almost inconceivably different from our own, and it will clearly be the case that humans that have the best capacity to *learn and adapt* and mould themselves to a new environment will survive, prosper and, therefore, reproduce. It should be noted that in a 'real world 'situation I don't even need to adapt to environments that are even physically plausible. For example what would happen to you, the reader, if you were suddenly teleported into the South American jungle and had to survive as a hunter-gatherer? The fact is that unless you were a very fast learner you would probably die (whereas EP would tend to predict that your pre-existing cognitive modules, which were specifically adapted for this environment, would 'kick in' and you would probably live). You have *learnt* to adapt to the environments that you are *likely* to find yourself in. It is simply false to say that you *need* to be able to adapt yourself to all possible environments.

Cosmides and Tooby go on to argue:

> That means that no cue could be used by the general decision rule, because a cue that is associated with one outcome in one environment will be associated with another outcome in another environment. By varying the structure of the environment, any cue could become associated with any outcome with equal probability, so no cue would ever be informative. A decision rule that gains no information from the environment can produce only random decisions – which would not maximize fitness in any environment, let alone in every environment.

Again we will note that, as with Pinker, highly important and complex arguments are 'zoomed past' at extremely high speed such that this reader at least has difficulty making complete sense of them. However, what Cosmides and Tooby seem to be arguing here is that, in an infinite universe 'any cue could become associated with any outcome with equal probability'. This is why they previously argued that, if the brain really had to adapt to an infinite amount of 'Universes' then it would simply be overloaded. And of course this is true. But as I argued above, the brain does not in fact, have to adapt to an infinite number of 'Universes': merely the ones we live in at the moment. And in this Universe (i.e. land, on the planet Earth, over the last 20,000 years or so) it is not the case that 'any cue could be associated with any outcome with equal probability.' Cosmides and Tooby give no examples here, which is illuminating, because what they are really arguing here is that (for example) if I drop something from a tree, or see a lion, or see a river, or any other 'cue', this could be associated with '*any*' outcome. But this is self-evidently false. There are patterns in our world, and we learn to read them fairly quickly. Whatever the presence of a lion 'leads to' it is unlikely to be anything good: so we quickly learn to stay away from lions, crocodiles and so forth. Freshwater rivers may lead to many things but they will almost always lead to fresh drinking water. And so on.

But the key point here is that it is the basic assumptions of cognitivism that forced, so to speak, Cosmides and Tooby into their vehement denial that 'general purpose' learning systems could ever exist in the brain. And, as we have seen, this attitude was originally stated with the 'debate' (or intellectual war might be a better phrase) between cognitivists and behaviourists.

This is not the only argument that Cosmides and Tooby have put forward as to why 'learning faculties' are unlikely to have been selected by natural selection: although it's a key one. The argument above attempts to prove that general learning mechanisms are actually impossible. Other arguments merely attempt to show that they are unlikely. For example:

> There are domains of human activity for which the evolutionarily appropriate information processing strategy is complex, and deviations from this strategy result in large fitness costs. An organism that relied on the vagaries of trial-and-error learning for such domains would be at a selective disadvantage. (Cosmides and Tooby, 1987: 285–286).

Putting aside the (false) assumption that cognition is information processing for a second, we should look at this sentence carefully. The argument here would seem to be: life is complex. If we had to sit down and work it all out, we would never get anything done. Therefore, 'people' that use simple algorithms to simply act would act quicker and get more things done than people who didn't, therefore they would be more likely to reproduce and etc. etc. etc. Moreover, they put forward the idea that that 'learning' incurs 'fitness costs'. In an absolute sense this is probably true, but then so does using simple information processing modules to solve complex social questions: that is, the risk that the module will give the 'wrong answer'. And, unlike a general purpose learning 'module' a simple module will be unable to 'learn from its mistakes'.

We should note in passing why Evolutionary Psychologists spend lots of time attempting to show that people and therefore their underlying 'cognitive mechanisms' are all basically the same. Because if they weren't, the theory wouldn't work. Imagine if people were different and all mating strategies were different. Clearly, no module could ever match itself to all these different scenarios, and a general purpose device would be better.

But in any case it's really all beside the point. We really have to pinch ourselves to remind ourselves: there is no computer at the moment that could, *conceivably*, duplicate human behaviour in terms of the complex human social environment. Cosmides, Tooby and Pinker clearly believe that it's just a matter of time until they do, but as we have seen, that's merely a matter of faith, not science. Until they do, the idea that any 'modular' or even 'information processing' approach to these actions could possibly be successful is merely a hypothesis and an unproven one at that.

However this does bring something to the fore: the extent to which (although this is implicit in their thinking rather than explicit) the frame/qualification/ramification problems that crippled cognitivism in the 1980s haunt the thinking of Cosmides and Tooby. Because it was these arguments, coupled with funding and other practical problems, which led to the second 'AI Winter' and the beginning of the end of the cognitivist hegemony (other factors being of course, the rise of connectionism, and the even more radical alternatives to cognitivism which we will look at in Chapter Seven). Therefore it is at least interesting that Cosmides and Tooby seem to think that EP can solve these problems, and, therefore, 'save' cognitivism.

So we see, yet again, that EP is not biology which has been given a psychological 'twist'. Instead it is a variety of cognitivist psychology which is using ideas taken from biology to 'save' cognitivism from two major threats: the threat posed by connectionism (which, amongst other things, views the brain as a general purpose information processor) and also the threat posed by the 'frame problem' type argument against GOFAI. (To repeat, this is implicit in the writings of Cosmides and Tooby, but made explicit in a text by Ketelaar and Todd entitled: *Framing Our Thoughts: Ecological Rationality as Evolutionary Psychology's Answer to the Frame Problem* (Ketelaar and Todd, 2001). So how do Ketelaar and Todd argue that EP can save cognitivism?

The short answer is that they don't, and the longer answer is their wonderfully clear and coherent article demonstrating the increasing difficulties EP is finding itself in. Ketelaar and Todd first go onto argue that instead of going through all the possibilities that face it (this is the frame problem, of course), the animal will probably use 'fast and dirty' broad ranging search strategies through the problem space instead. This is probably true, but what has this got to do with cognitivism, and, therefore EP? The key problem is that it is precisely such 'fast and dirty' searches that traditional cognitivist models find so difficult to model (connectionist models using 'fuzzy logic' are much more successful). Simply saying 'and here, evolution steps in' is simply a Deus ex Machina: an attempt to use Darwin to plug gaps in a theory that isn't working. Modellers of traditional AI have been attempting to model human search strategies in problem space for years, to repeat, success only started to come when they began to ditch cognitivist orthodoxy and moved towards connectionist models or the even more radical modelling in the tradition of Rodney Brooks. The solution of 'pre-installed programming' is merely an attempt to offload the problem, so to speak onto natural selection. The key point is not whether or not the behaviour was caused by 'pre-installed' programming or not: the key point is, was it caused by programming at all? And if we begin to answer that the answer to this question is 'yes' then we run into all the problems that cognitivism always runs into (the Chinese Room, the frame problem, the homunculus problem).

The second solution that Ketelaar and Todd bring out is to use emotion as a 'differentiating device' (i.e. a way of 'weighting' the correct 'path' in problem space). Again, it is unquestionably true that this is how things work in the real world, but one of the key cognitivist assumptions is on the difference between 'rationality' (based on logic) and 'irrationality' (based on emotion and un-modelable in cognitivist models). Indeed, the introduction of the study of emotion into psychology has been one of the key factors for straight forward cognitivism to go out of fashion! (We shall again explore this issue further in chapter seven). Again, thinkers in EP are simply trying to have their cake and eat it: introducing ideas that are incompatible with cognitivism into cognitivist models and hoping no one will notice because of the Darwinian rhetoric being used to 'cover their tracks'.

Therefore the attempt won't work. Cognitivism, even in it EP guise, still cannot answer the questions posed by the frame problem and similar problems.

Learning

Underlying much of EP rhetoric is the idea that learning ('the vagaries of trial and error learning') is an extraordinarily complex, difficult and boring task, which anyone in their right mind would avoid if they could ('large fitness costs'). But of course (*of course*) learning can be fun. Moreover, self-evidently, learning can lead to an adaptive advantage, not just in survival, but also in terms of attractiveness to a mate. Moreover, any fitness *costs* that are incurred must be balanced by the fitness *advantages* of being able to adapt to a wide variety of situations.

Finally for these arguments to make sense, EP tends to hold that for some ('complex') human activities there is one, and one only, appropriate strategy and to deviate from this strategy would 'incur fitness costs'. And which human activities are these, one might ask? Cosmides and Tooby provide answers that relate to another issue (which, again, we will look at later), these issues relate to mating, and other social phenomena that arose in the Pleistocene. But, again, is this true? Is it true that there is one, and one only, strategy that will gain a partner with whom we can reproduce? If people are essentially the same, everywhere and in all periods of time, then obviously the answer might be 'yes'. But if this does not hold then the idea of one strategy fits all falls down, and yet again, we find that a learning, or 'trial and error' mechanism makes a lot more sense.

Putting aside the (bizarre) belief that we 'evolved for' the Pleistocene and that ever since our poor brains have been desperate to get back there[7] we see why the anthropological discoveries of the last century which have shown the great variance in human behaviour are so threatening to EP: if these reports are true then, essentially, EP could not be. The concept of discrete, static, pre-programmed information processing modules which we are born with, only makes sense if 'human nature' is essentially the same: everywhere and at all times. Hence EP's unlovely tendency not so much to *explain* anthropological data as to *explain it away.* How does EP explain the vast multiplicity in human behaviours shown by anthropology across times and cultures? The answer is it doesn't and can't. And so, when this evidence is produced, instead of changing the theory to fit the data, EPers tend to dismiss the data to fit the theory. Anyone who discovers societies which are radically different from our own must be mistaken, or politically motivated, or something of that sort. And this follows from the original approach of cognitivism which of course, was reasoned from *a priori* grounds, not on the basis of empirical evidence. Cognitivists believed that their 'theories' were true *by definition*. And EP follows in that tradition.

---

7 To test the accuracy of this prediction: there are still 'primitive' hunter-gatherer tribes in South America and a few other places. The reader may if s/he wishes fly out to these places and parachute into these tribes. Let me know if you feel 'at home' in these places. Send me a postcard.

Schank and Case Based Learning

Just as, as we will see, scientists in the EP tradition wildly overstate the influence and longevity of what they call the Standard Social Science Model (essentially, behaviourism) of human cognition and behaviour, cognitivists also wildly overstate the popularity of cognitivism. And in both cases, the reasons for this should be obvious. However it would be wise to have a reality check here, and remind ourselves of just what cognitivism was (past tense very much intended) and how much sway it had in various academic departments.

Behaviourism, it's true, was pretty influential in early 20th century psychology but it was by no means the only game in town. Freudian psychoanalysis and its various offshoots (Jungian thought, Adlerian psychology, Reichian thought and so forth) were also extremely popular. In Germany there was the Gestalt school and in France the school of developmental psychology that developed from Piaget.

Chomskyan linguistics began to be developed in the mid nineteen fifties, but it was not until a good ten years later that it began to be influential on psychology, and, as we have noted, it was not then and is not now the dominant school in linguistics. It was not until the mid nineteen sixties that what has begun to be called the 'cognitive revolution' really began to get going, but even here we should not overstate its popularity. To begin with, cognitivism has only really been influential in psychology. In economics, archaeology, sociology and the other social sciences its influence has been marginal, and even when it has been influential this has mainly been in terms of the increasing use of phrases like 'information processing' in a highly loose and metaphorical sense, not in the sense of cognitivism's key tenets: i.e. that thought is the manipulation of symbols by rules in internal cognitive space. In philosophy the Computational Theory of Mind was popular in the 1950s and 1960s but by the nineteen seventies under the influence of philosophers like Hubert Dreyfus as well as the revival of pragmatism the pendulum began to swing back. Moreover, as we have seen, the two leading functionalist philosophers Hilary Putnam and Jerry Fodor both 'recanted' in the 1980s (Fodor to a certain extent, and Putnam to a much greater extent). In any case Fodor has always been profoundly hostile to EP. In artificial intelligence itself, thinkers in the so called GOFAI tradition are now in the process of being usurped by more modern thinkers like Brooks as we shall see.

However, it's fair to say that cognitivism became more and more influential throughout the 1970s and by the 1980s was probably the most influential school in British and American psychology (Continental Europeans have always been more sceptical and Eastern Bloc psychology at the time was dominated by Activity Theory, which was profoundly hostile to cognitivist assumptions). Nevertheless even here it was not unchallenged. For example, the tradition of Ecological Psychology which derived from the thought of J.J. Gibson also flourished, and has continued to provide a challenge to the cognitivist orthodoxy (see later).

Another one of the key opposing intellectual currents to cognitivism in the mid to late seventies was Case Based Reasoning a theory proposed by Roger Schank. Some people might be surprised to see Schank mentioned in opposition to cognitivism, as he was, generally speaking, in favour of the information processing approach to cognition and also because he was a strong proponent of AI. Nonetheless, Schank proposed a model of learning that was significantly different from that of 'classic' cognitivism (as was evinced by some famously acrimonious debates he had with Noam Chomsky) and will help us to see why the idea that learning by 'trial and error' is *necessarily* a complex and time consuming activity is false.

Schank suggested that instead of a library of *rules* (algorithms) the mind/brain actually consists of a library of *cases*. Now presumably these 'cases' were still controlled and accessed by rules: Schank was not that much of a rebel. Nonetheless it did shift learning theory back to a new emphasis on empiricism, and also provided a model to help explain how learning actually happens (extraordinarily enough, cognitivists have no real theory as to how learning occurs, which is why they tend to minimise its importance) (Riesbeck and Schank, 1989).

Schank posited the idea that as we grow up we encounter certain situations which are then stored in the brain: and most people would agree with this. However Schank then went on to posit the idea that when facing a new situation, instead of simply approaching it afresh, we will instead tend to adapt a previous situation which we already know how to deal with to see whether or not it will 'fit' the new situation. For example, say we have never been to a restaurant before. How can we learn how to order food? According to EP, this will be an incredibly complex (and hence, unlikely) process of 'trial and error'. But of course what Schank pointed out is that even though we may never have been in a restaurant before, we will have been in other situations that are *a bit like* being in a restaurant before. For example, we already have, 'stored' in our brain, the knowledge of how to eat food off a table, how to eat with a knife and fork, how to drink from a glass. Moreover, we have previous, case based, experience of how to buy things for money. And we, presumably have been in a shop before. OK: none of these are precisely the same as being in a restaurant, but we can draw on these cases and adapt them to this new experience. When faced with a new situation we do not have to start from 'first principles': we can draw on previous experience.

There are two things to say about this theory: first, unlike cognitivist theories of learning (note: strictly speaking this is a contradiction in terms. The appeal of cognitivist nativism is that it seemed to get rid of the need for a theory of learning, instead, explaining almost all human activity in terms of the behaviour of modules which we are born with) there is a lot of empirical evidence to back up Schank's theories (For example, Klein and Calderwood, 1988).

And secondly, it explains why Cosmides and Tooby's arguments in favour of massive modularity are wrong. To repeat their argument: 'There are domains of human activity for which the evolutionarily appropriate information processing strategy is complex, and deviations from this strategy result in large fitness costs.' Schank points out that deviations from common strategies are in fact the way we normally think, and do not in fact incur huge fitness costs, as they are adaptions of pre-existing cognitive strategies.

Schank's Cased Based Learning was an alternative to cognitivist proper, but as noted still stayed within the basic cognitivist framework. A much bigger threat to the cognitivist orthodoxy appeared in 1986 when Rumelhart and McClelland produced their masterpiece *Parallel Distributed Processing: Explorations in the Micro-structure of Cognition.*

We first touched on connectionism in chapter one, when we looked at Marvin Minsky, and there is no particular need to go into the basics of connectionism here. Suffice to say that connectionism is an attempt to model the human brain with electronic 'versions' of neurons (Pinker calls them 'toy neurons'). Instead of the usual symbols and rules, these 'nodes' interact with each other in a 'spreading' wave of 'activation'. The relationships thereby produced are statistical and probabilistic (analogue) rather than the digital approach of classical cognitivism.

Now, despite the hopeful term 'neural networks' that is sometimes attached to these connectionism networks, as Pinker rightly points out these networks are at present far less sophisticated than the human brain. Nevertheless, they are still an attempt to model it: and in that sense, they at least acknowledge the fact that the brain is a biological (not computational) artefact.

This is one of the reasons Pinker does not like connectionism but it's not the main one. The main reason he doesn't like it, as he puts it: 'a ... network is a high-tech implementation of an ancient doctrine, the association of ideas ... association ... was also thought to be the scrivener that fills the famous blank slate ... the blank slate and the ... general purpose laws of learning are also the psychological underpinnings of the Standard Social Science Model' (Pinker, 2003: 113). And, one might add, behaviourism. And if behaviourism was true, of course cognitivism could not be. In other words, Pinker sees connectionism as a return to behaviourism.

It's not, however, that Pinker completely junks the whole idea. Instead, he posits the idea that connectionism could solve the 'homunculus' problem that we met earlier: perhaps connectionist 'toy neurons' could be the basic nodes flashing on and off that would 'decompose' the homunculus? Therefore the brain would be a symbolic cognitivist digital computer, floating on top of, so to speak, a connectionist base.

Let's leave aside for a second as to whether or not that will even work. But the key point is that connectionists are not, on the whole, content with this half way house 'truce'. They don't want a slice of the pie: they want the whole pie. So connectionists have increasingly been 'muscling in' on cognitivist territory. This has lead to a rather ironic reversal of fortune. It is now the cognitivists who are the Luddites, stating all the things that connectionist networks 'can't do' (in the same way as opponents of GOFAI used to list all the things that digital computers couldn't do). And when these things are done, then new challenges are conjured up.

And of course, this contest might go on forever: or at least a very long time. It's highly unlikely that connectionist networks will ever fully mimic successfully the human brain, and even if they do, it will take a very long time: decades, possibly even centuries. But that's not the point. We aren't talking artificial intelligence here, and its possibly quixotic quest to create a walking, talking, conscious robot or computer. Instead we are talking about science, and whether or not connectionist networks are effective tools for modelling the human brain, albeit in a simplified form.

And to this question (are connectionist models useful and accurate models for the scientific study of the brain, albeit in simplified form) connectionists would of course say 'yes'. And, increasingly, they are rejecting the 'truce' offered by the cognitivists, whereby it is granted that 'subconscious' or 'neural' phenomena are connectionist, but 'high level' cognition must always be modelled with cognitivist models. Connectionists increasingly wonder whether *all* neural phenomena can be modelled with connectionist models. This would of course make cognitivism simply redundant.

Five Arguments Against Connectionism

Pinker obviously perceives this as a very serious threat, as he devotes no less than fourteen pages to attacking connectionism in *How the Mind Works*: and he is right to do so. To repeat, he is not attacking connectionism *per se*. What he is attacking is the idea that connectionism, as a theory of mind, could ever replace cognitivism, or the 'symbolic' hypothesis.

Pinker has five main arguments, of which two are so to speak 'absolutist' arguments (i.e. demonstrations that connectionism could never work as a 'total' theory of mind) and three empirical arguments. We will look at the 'absolutist' arguments first, and I think it will become apparent quite quickly that they are actually the same argument.

The first feat that, apparently, cognitivism can explain that connectionism can't, is the concept of an individual. To quote Pinker: 'Rather than symbolizing an entity as an arbitrary pattern in a string of bits (i.e. as in cognitivism), we represented it as a pattern in a layer of units (i.e. connectionism), each standing for one of the entity's properties. An immediate problem is that there is no longer a way to tell apart two individuals with identical properties'. (Pinker, 2003:115). But of course this depends what you mean by the word 'identical'. If two things are literally identical then of course there *is* no way to tell them apart, in any philosophy of mind. But that's not what Pinker means: he means identical 'to all intents and purposes'. And he is also not talking about our pragmatic ability to understand that thing are different but our ability to understand the concept of 'difference'. But so what? Why should this necessitate cognitivism? In reality, two things that are identical (for example, chairs, as in Pinker's example) have not only different physical properties but different histories and different uses. There really is no such thing as two large objects which are *literally* identical and our ability to understand this concept says more about our powers of imagination than anything else ... imagination being a human faculty that cognitivism has particular difficulty with.

And even if this was not the case, as Pinker rightly points out, we can understand things as being different even though they look the same by virtue of the fact that they are in different spatial locations (even if we are looking at two chairs which look similar, we are unlikely to come to the conclusion that we are looking at one chair not two). But Pinker has an answer to this point.

> Suppose an infinite white plain contains nothing but two identical circles. One of them slides over and superimposes itself on the second one for a few moments, then proceeds on its way. I don't think anyone has trouble conceiving of the circles as distinct entities, even in the moments where they are in the same place at the same time. (Pinker, 2003: 116).

But this makes no sense. Pinker is implying that the 'world' of the 'plane' is 2-D, like in Edwin Abbott's novel *Flatland*. But if that is the case, then clearly one circle *can't* superimpose itself on anything as superimposition needs the dimension of height. And if it's a 3-D world, then clearly a circle superimposing itself on another circle is NOT the same as 'being in the same place at the same time', just as if I put a chair on top of a table, they are not 'in the same place at the same time'. People have only an abstract notion of things being identical, not an empirical one, because in reality, there is no such thing as a (larger than sub-atomic, perceivable) object *being literally identical* to another, and so the fact that in connectionism we have difficulty expressing that concept is irrelevant.

The next argument is really the same argument phrased differently. Pinker argues that fuzzy (or analogue, qualitative) logic (which connectionist models can mimic well) is all very well. But sometimes we also use digital, quantitative categorisation. And digital thinking is something that, naturally enough, a digital, cognitivist computer can do very well. And he uses the example of the joke 'you can't be a little bit pregnant'. This is true enough to an extent, but it's also true that these 'digital categories' can be easily shaken. After all, the whole abortion debate is really an argument about whether or not you *can* be a 'little bit pregnant', in a meaningful sense: i.e. pregnant with a human infant. There has been a huge amount of empirical data that people's categorisation systems are really a lot more fuzzy than the 'digital' model suggested by Pinker (Rosch, 1978). And in any case, connectionist networks can *learn*. Again, this is why Pinker dislikes them. Pinker goes on to quote Hinton, Rumelhart and McClelland 'If for example you learn that chimpanzees like onions you will probably raise your estimate of the probability that chimpanzees like onions.' (Pinker, 2003: 128). After a long passage in which Pinker argues that he, Pinker, would never think such a thing, Pinker then admits that connectionist networks would make this mistake 'unless it is trained': i.e. unless it learns. But that's the whole point. Connectionist networks *do* learn. They can learn anything a 'cognitivist' model can learn. There is no need to argue (as the cognitivists do) that people must be *born* knowing this that or the other.

Pinker knows this but he then has another card to play: talking of another connectionist model which takes quite a long time to understand about family relationships, he begins his rebuttal 'obviously …': the implication being that human beings 'wouldn't have the time' to learn such things.[8] To which one can only reply: well *who says* it's obvious that humans would not have the time to learn things this way? If this argument sounds familiar, it's because it is. It's the 'poverty of the stimulus' argument again. And if one will forgive me here (but it's too tempting not to play this particular card) Pinker, here sounds like nothing so much as the creationist playing what Richard Dawkins calls the 'argument from incredulity'. 'Obviously', Pinker continually argues, 'no one' could possibly have the time to learn X, therefore … cognitivism!

---

8   Of course here one must pinch oneself and be reminded that in the real world it is cognitivist, not connectionist, models that have intense problems with adapting to real world situations in real time, because of the frame problem.

But this is based on the cognitivist presupposition that learning is something we do only occasionally, that we find it very hard, that it is inefficient and so forth. But as I have argued, this view really derives from cognitivist hostility to behaviourism. If one follows the logic of what I have argued is conventional Darwinism and assume that the brain is a general purpose learning device then these objections vanish. If all we do is learn, from the moment we are born to the day we die 'morning noon and night', then obviously both the 'time' and 'effort' objections fall by the wayside.

Pinker's other objections are empirical and again of the 'argument from incredulity' variety. He argues that connectionist networks will never be able to produce 'compositionality, quantification, and recursion' or that if they can it's only because they mimic cognitivist models. What these are needn't concern us here. What should concern us is that this is Pinker's own very partial statement of what connectionist networks 'can't do'. It must be stated clearly that connectionists themselves do not accept Pinker's self-proscribed strictures on what they 'can't do', and argue that connectionist networks can do all these things just fine (Aizawa, 1997). Some also go on to argue that some of the cognitivist's arguments are so strong that their conclusion is not only that connectionist networks couldn't do these things, but cognitivist models couldn't either! (Chalmers, 1991). Clearly something has gone very wrong here: the bar is being set too high. As Pinker grudgingly puts it: 'By training the living daylights out of a generic hidden-layer network one can sometimes get it to do approximately the right thing' (Pinker, 1999: 130). But of course one might add 'by training the living daylights out of an athlete one can sometimes get him or her to run fast…but never as fast or as efficiently as a car. Therefore, merely training or learning must be a substitute for the human being's internal combustion engine …'. The key point of course (OF COURSE) is that in the real world people enjoy learning, find the time for it, and find many evolutionary advantages (in terms of attractiveness, survival skills etc.) flow from learning, and the speed and ability with which they can learn. This is not the solution to the problem but it is part of the solution.

What's going on here, of course, is that Pinker *et al.* can't get over the fact that they are no longer 'the new boys in town'. Despite his youthful good looks and self-consciously 'controversial' opinions, Pinker is not an enfant terrible. He is the establishment and what happens to establishment thinkers is they get challenged by younger, more radical colleagues. Indeed, Pinker on connectionism sounds like nothing so much as those anti-cognitivist thinkers in the 1950s and 1960s who mocked GOFAI by arguing that digital computers would 'never' be able to do X, Y, or Z. The problem for Pinker is that the connectionist revolution is likely to be a far more broad reaching and radical one than the cognitivist one. In a thoughtful but devastating review of Pinker's *Words and Rules,* McClelland and Mark Seidenberg argued that:

> Pinker's analysis of the formation of the English past tense is reminiscent of the astronomer Tycho Brahe's attempt to come to terms with Copernican theory. Tycho formulated a compromise that captured some of the appeal of the Copernican approach, while maintaining the key Ptolemaic principle of geocentrism. Correspondingly, Pinker has seen some of the appeal of the neural network approach, and he has found ways to incorporate elements of it in a compromise position that maintains the key principle that language knowledge consists (at least in part) of rules. He relies on the properties of neural networks to address problems with the traditional rules-plus-words point of view. His resistance to the core tenets of the neural network framework, however, leaves him – like Tycho – with a compromise that really deals only partially with the challenge posed by the emerging system.
>
> Thus it may be fitting that *Words and Rules* appears at the end of the old millennium. Written amidst an ongoing research debate, it captures a transitional mode of thought that may be typical of a scientific revolution in progress. Pinker supplies an engaging treatment of an attempt to find a middle ground between two incommensurate theoretical frameworks, and he provides numerous entries to the stream of ongoing research in which the full potential of the newer, neural network

> approach will eventually become apparent. (McLelland and Seidenberg, 2000)

This nicely makes clear one of the basic points of this book: rather than being a bold, innovative, 21st century science, EP is essentially a reactionary attempt to 'patch up' 20th century cognitivist orthodoxy, in the face of connectionism and the even newer approaches that are rapidly changing the face of modern psychology.

Brain Science

There is one final point to be made, and, again, it is conceptual, which is: is EP actually physically possible?

As we have seen, EP shared with cognitivism and functionalism a disdain for neuro-psychology, arguing that it simply 'didn't matter' what 'hardware' the mind (conceptualised as 'software') 'ran on'. This led to some weird conclusions, drawn out by the philosopher Ned Block in his idea of the 'China Brain'. (Block, 1980). In this thought experiment, Block asks that we imagine that every citizen of China, either by using walkie-talkies, or telephones, or whatever, simulates the actions of neurons. In other words, China begins to function as giant brain. The question is: 'is China conscious?'.

According to the functionalists the answer really has to be 'yes', even though this seems like a really strange thing to say, and Block has argued that just because it seems so weird this in itself is a sign that something has gone wrong with the cognitivist/functionalist 'it's not the hardware it's the software' argument.

What is not in doubt is that in some absolute sense, software must be implementable on compatible hardware. You can't run Windows Vista on a ZX Spectrum (or a pocket calculator). There must be some link, no matter how tenuous, between the capabilities of the hardware and the functions of the software.

Massive modularity, clearly, needs a brain that can support static, discrete or semi-discrete information processing modules, and is far more 'devoted to' modularity than learning. This was a brain model that seemed plausible when cognitivism was first proposed. But it's not plausible anymore. The discovery of neuroplasticity (Dodge, 2007) demonstrates that the brain is 'plastic' to an extent almost unsuspected 50 years ago, the brain is almost constantly 'rewiring itself' (i.e. learning). Even more radically, the discovery of neuro-genesis (Gould *et al.*, 1999) shows that the brain can generate new neurons, even, perhaps, quite late into life. The brain is not in any sense 'static'. And yet a 'static brain' is what the massive modularity thesis would seem to require.

And is the brain modular anyway? Michael Shermer writes: 'University of California, San Diego, philosopher of the mind Patricia S. Churchland told me with unabashed scepticism: "Mental modules are complete nonsense. There are no modules that are encapsulated and just send information into a central processor. There are areas of specialization, yes, and networks maybe, but these are not always dedicated to a particular task." Instead of mental module metaphors, *let us use neural networks*.' (Shermer, 2008). (Note: neural networks are another name for connectionist models). Indeed, Deacon, (1997) argues that cognitivist models are simply *impossible* in terms of what we now know about the brain. Whatever one thinks of this, it is not good news for EP.

So, if EP is dead, with what should we replace it? It is this question that the next chapter will answer.

Chapter Seven

How the Mind Works

Cognitivism achieved its success in the 1970s and early 1980s because it was seen as being the 'only game in town'. And even now, opponents of cognitivism (and it must be stressed that EP is merely cognitivism with, so to speak, Darwinian bells on) are often challenged with the question: 'Well, if cognitivism isn't true, how do *you* explain consciousness/cognition/thinking, then?'

But this is self-evidently not fair. It is not incumbent on me to explain how the mind works, as I'm not making that claim. It wasn't me that wrote a book called *How the Mind Works*: it was Steven Pinker. The burden of proof doesn't fall on me to prove my claims: it falls in him to prove his. And in any case, it's not true (as cognitivists tend to imply) that any kind of theory, even a terrible one, is better than no theory at all. In the early stages of any science (and psychology in the Western sense, as a subject taught at Western universities, is still quite new) it is usually better merely to gather evidence and wait and see what happens. A bad theory can actually hold up progress by concentrating minds on irrelevant research questions, and acting as barrier to new ideas (due to academic inertia). It is arguable that cognitivism has not been helpful in this regard.

So even if no one had any idea of how the mind/brain works, it still wouldn't prove a single one of cognitivism's theories. But actually things aren't quite that bleak. Indeed, since 1986, and the publication of Rumelhart and McClelland's masterwork *Parallel Distributed Processing: Explorations in the Micro-Structure of Cognition* there has been a growing groundswell of opinion that cognitivist orthodoxy should and, now, can be challenged, and replaced with better and more accurate models of cognition.

The Collapse of GOFAI

They key point here is GOFAI. As was pointed out earlier, it was vital to the cognitivist enterprise that digital computers could be shown to mimic the behaviour of 'higher level' human cognitive features, otherwise the whole project would simply become an interesting metaphor: poetic, perhaps, but hardly science.

But GOFAI did not do well in the 1990s. Even by 1990, computer scientist Rodney Brooks could write:

> Artificial Intelligence research has foundered in a sea of incrementalism. No one is quite sure where to go save improving on earlier demonstrations of techniques in *symbolic manipulation of ungrounded representations*. At the same time, small AI companies are folding, and attendance is well down at national and international Artificial Intelligence conferences. While it is true that the use of AI is prospering in many large companies, it is primarily through the application to novel domains of long developed techniques that have become passé in the research community. What has gone wrong?
>
> In this paper we argue that the *symbol system hypothesis* upon which *classical AI is* based is fundamentally flawed, and as such imposes severe limitations on the fitness of its progeny. Further, we argue that the dogma of the symbol system hypothesis implicitly includes a number of largely unfounded great leaps of faith when called upon to provide a plausible path to the digital equivalent of human level intelligence. It

is the chasms to be crossed by these leaps which now impede classical AI Research. (Brooks, 1990: 3).

If the phrase 'symbol system' sounds familiar, it should. 'Symbol system' is simply another phrase for cognitivism. And what Brooks wrote came to pass: increasingly, throughout the 1990s, 'symbolic' AI began to be seen as a 'busted flush'. To echo Brooks: what went wrong? As we have seen, the so-called, cognitive revolution was a 'revolution' against behaviourism onto which, so to speak, a classic Western debate, between rationalism and empiricism, was foisted. This is not the whole truth, but it's undoubtedly correct that cognitivism owes *something* to Rationalism in the same way that behaviourism (and connectionism, and Schank's theories) owe *something* to Empiricism. And Rationalism is, as one might think, the idea that cognition 'is' rationality, and rationality is then defined as being mathematical or logical in nature (we have seen this view in Chomsky and others). It is this view that Brooks was challenging. Rather than *facilitating* AI, as had generally been assumed, Brooks began to argue that cognitivism was *holding AI back*, and that only by ditching it could real progress be made. If Cognitivism is false as a description of human cognition (and it is) then, self-evidently, AI would never make progress as long as it adopted its tenets.

And so Brooks, like other thinkers in the field, began to turn away to cognitivism, first, as we have seen, to connectionism, but then to even more radical approaches, which have been termed 'The New Psychology' or 'Postcognitivism'

The New Psychology

What is the 'New Psychology' (Wallace, 2006)? To begin with there is the problem of 'what to call it'. At the moment there is no generally agreed upon term. Some call this new approach 'enactivism', a phrase popularised by the neurophysiologists Maturana and Varela (Varela *et al.*, 1991). Others have concentrated on specific aspects of the new approach: for example, the ungainly acronym 4EA (for 'Embodied, Embedded, Enactive, Extended, Affective' psychology). Others choose to concentrate on other aspects of the new approach: situated cognition, embodied cognition, discursive psychology, distributed cognition.

Whatever phrase one uses, the 'new psychology' is both more modest and more challenging than the (now fading) cognitivist orthodoxy. It is more modest because, unlike cognitivism, the 'new psychologists' do not simply hysterically deny the value of all previous movements in psychology. There are no scathing denunciations of the anti-scientific nature of cognitivism in the new literature, in the way that the cognitivists viciously denounced behaviourists. On the contrary, the new psychologists acknowledge the experimental (and other) findings of cognitivists and (whisper it!) behaviourists, all the while stressing that the key problem is not the empirical data itself, but the theoretical framework in which the data is interpreted.

However, make no mistake, the new psychology is also more radical than either cognitivism or behaviourism, because it attempts to undercut the assumptions that lie behind them both.[1] There are two major assumptions that lie behind cognitivism *and* behaviourism: the assumption that the human being is fundamentally passive, and the various dualisms that both approaches accept as 'givens.'[2]

---

1 It's outwith the scope of this discussion, but one might also add 'and the assumptions that both have in common with psycho-analysis'. Despite its seeming 'radicalness' psycho-analysis has a traditional Western emphasis on the individual's psychology, and the are other similarities as well.

2 Vincent Descombes: 'Today's mentalist (i.e. cognitivist) philosophy relies on the same conception of observable conduct as does the behaviourism it is at such pains to denounce: that behaviour is a physical phenomenon whose cause must be sought. But it has the same conception of this cause as did the mentalist philosophy: that this cause is a mental process.' (Descombes, 2001: 19).

Cybernetics

It is in its rejection of the first of these assumptions that the New Psychology sounds most different from cognitivism/ behaviourism. As we have seen, these views derived from the desire to make psychology 'scientific', by which was meant, 'based on Newtonian physics'. And this therefore meant that both cognitivists and behaviourists were committed to stimulus-response or stimulus-cognition-response (i.e. cause-effect). Therefore both cognitivists and behaviourists were committed to the idea that human beings are fundamentally *passive* (a view, shared, interestingly enough, by psychologists in the Freudian tradition).

But this view is self-evidently ridiculous, and an alternative view was propounded by John Dewey as early as 1896, in his classic essay *The Reflex Arc Concept in Psychology* (Dewey, 1896). Dewey pointed out in this essay that the simple 'stimulus-response' concept was ridiculously simplistic when applied to humans (or animals, for that matter). Instead, he proposed a 'reflex arc' in which the stimulus caused a response *but which then went on to provoke a new stimulus and so on:* in other words, a feedback loop. Now this reference to a feedback loop is deliberate as it brings us to the science of cybernetics, which to a certain extent recapitulated what Dewey had discovered. Cybernetics is the science of control systems, and it gives us the clearest and most explicit description of feedback and control systems. Gary Cziko gives us a clear demonstration of what this might mean, in the most humble of contexts.

> The modern flush toilet must have a certain amount of water on hand for each flush to be effective. For this purpose, most residential toilets make use of a holding tank into which water accumulates between flushes. Since too little water in the tank does not allow adequate flushing and too much is wasteful (it will simply flow out through an overflow drain), a mechanism is used to maintain the water at the desired level.
>
> This mechanism consists of a float resting on the surface of the water that is connected to a valve. When the water level falls after a flush, the float falls with it and in so doing opens

a valve, admitting water into the tank. But as the tank fills and the water level rises, so does the float, eventually closing the valve so that the tank does not overfill.

For the reader who has not already peered inside a flush toilet tank, it is well worth lifting the lid and taking a look. With the tank lid off and the flush lever activated, one can observe in live action the events described: the tank empties, the float falls, the valve turns on, the tank refills, and the valve shuts off. It is also informative to push lightly on the flush lever for a few seconds so that just a portion of the water in the tank escapes into the bowl. This will show that the tank need not be emptied completely before the float valve mechanism acts to refill the tank. If all is operating properly, the float-valve mechanism will not let the water remain very much below the desired level.

What is this desired level? Inside most tanks a line indicates the optimal amount of water for flushing the toilet. If the water level in your tank is above or below this line, it can be changed by adjusting the float's position on the link that connects it to the valve. By changing the distance between the float and the valve, you can control the water level that will be reached before the valve turns itself off (Cziko, 2000: 60–61).

Not the most illuminating of examples it might seem, but actually something very interesting is going on here, as Cziko continues:

Notice the phrase I used in the preceding sentence — 'the valve turns itself off.' Is this actually the case? Isn't it rather that the rising float causes the valve to close? Yes, of course. But what is it that causes the float to rise? Obviously, the water that is filling the tank. And why is the water entering the tank? Because the valve is open. And what will cause the valve to close? The rising water level. So the valve, through a series of events, does in a sense close itself, since the valve's opening eventually causes it to close again. If it seems that we are going around in a circle here, it is because we are. (Cziko, 2000: 61).

This is the world of cybernetics feedback loops or reflex arcs, and it is a world where *things cause themselves to do things*. As the example of the toilet shows, there is absolutely nothing mystical or religious about this concept: it is merely what certain kind of control systems do. But it gives us a hint as to how material objects can be *active*, not passive. Systems like flush toilets, cruise control in a car, or air conditioners. Moreover, not only do these systems cause themselves to do something but due to the fact that they seek homeostasis (or the mid point in the flush toilet example above) they also have purpose: teleology. It is a derived purpose to be sure, but nevertheless it is now not too difficult to see how natural selection could have created such a thing and how purpose can arise from blind materialist forces.

Does this 'cybernetic' theory approximate human behaviour more closely than cognitivist models? Sheer common sense might insist that the answer must be 'yes': the cognitivist/ behaviourist view of human beings as being fundamentally passive was always absurd, although it fitted in well with their attempt make psychology a branch of physics (a 'passive' human psychology would of course make humans more similar to other simple objects like stones or bricks, and hence easier to model, mathematically). However, there is other evidence that is relevant here.

To see what this is we must return to the work of Boris Kotchoubey. Kotchoubey tested the human P3 'brain wave', which is associated with 'higher level' (i.e. conscious, cognitive) thought. Now, what 'should' happen in the cognitivist/ behaviourist paradigm is that, when given a stimulus, there should be a (very) brief pause, then a P3 wave (cognition) then a behaviour (response). For example, if I prick your skin with a needle, then I am, so to speak, 'introducing' information to your brain (via the nerves in your skin), so there should then be a P3 wave while my brain 'processes' this information, and then a response (you go 'Ow!' or whatever).

But this is not what happens. Indeed, Kotchoubey found numerous examples in human volunteers of the P3 wave occurring *before* the stimulus. Of course this has occurred before and usually gets explained away by cognitivists as 'preattentive cognition' or some other euphemism.

But this only makes sense if the stimulus actually occurs. What happens if it doesn't? What is 'pre' about the 'preattentive cognition' *then*? Kotchoubey argues that abstruse phraseology is being used here to cover up the fact that cognition can happen without a stimulus. The basic 'stimulus-cognition-response' model is simply not accurate as a model of human behaviour. (Kotchoubey and Lang, 2001).[3]

Dualisms

An even more fundamental problem with cognitivism, however, and a more subtle one, is cognitivism's recapitulation of Cartesian Dualism: the split between Body and Mind. Here Vincent Descombes puts it neatly: 'It is today considered 'good form' to declare that Cartesian Dualism has been overcome. Yet experience shows that *declarations are not enough*' (Descombes, 2001: 10). (italics added). Descombes is right. One could hardly get taken seriously nowadays as a 'cutting edge' cognitive scientist without, at some point, declaring that Dualism is Dead (or something similar). Indeed, in *The Blank Slate*, Steven Pinker spends much time by arguing against the idea of the Ghost in the Machine, a phrase coined, let's not forget, by Gilbert Ryle, a behaviourist philosopher. But of course merely *saying* 'we are now past dualism' isn't enough. You have to actually do it. For example, one would have to show that one's own theory of mind is not only explicitly but implicitly, so to speak, anti-dualist, and that dualism has not been 'smuggled in via the back door'. Moreover one would have to demonstrate that, even if this particular Dualism has been destroyed, other dualisms had not quickly taken its place: for example a dualism between the 'inner' and the 'outer', or between the individual and the social.

---

3 Of course many cognitivists would claim that they have 'gone beyond' stimulus-response thinking, but as Hebb once pointed out: 'the whole meaning of the term "cognitive" depends on [the stimulus-response idea], though cognitive psychologists seem unaware of the fact' ((Hebb, 1960: 737).

This is important because I would argue that Cognitivism is, in fact, committed to Cartesian Dualism (as Noam Chomsky would of course be the first to admit). The Cartesian Dualism of Cognitivism is well hidden, but no less profound for all that. Because the fact is that once one has started to talk about 'two kinds of stuff': material stuff, 'caused' by the laws of physics, and 'information stuff' 'caused' by the laws of logic, then one is implicitly talking a Dualistic kind of language, but one which *seems* to be 'Monist'(in this case, materialist). As Vincent Descombes puts it:

> The analogy (i.e. of the brain) with the computer is at the heart of the new mentalist philosophy because it *seems* to offer a solution to this problem (i.e. the problem of combining materialism with Cartesianism). It presents us with a machine that can be described in two ways: *as if it were* a Cartesian composite made up of a thinking system and a material system but that *we know to be nothing but* a material system. Such a model combines all the advantages of the mentalist doctrine (the mind is dissociated from the world) and the naturalist doctrine (the human person is made up of only one substance and not two) (Descombes, 2001, p. 110: Note: by 'the new mentalist psychology' Descombes means cognitivism. Words inside brackets added; emphasis as original).

The 'magic trick' here is to posit the world of information as an 'autonomous realm', with a *de facto* freedom from the basic laws of matter but which (just as with a digital computer) is 'in fact' and 'ultimately' governed by the same laws *as* matter.

But as we have seen the trick won't work, because the world of information is not only not autonomous in the sense posited by cognitivism, actually it isn't autonomous *in any sense*. It *seems* to be autonomous in our computers because in our computers, human beings with minds build the computers, program the computers and run the programs. So it makes sense, in this context, to speak of 'hardware' and 'software': because we can forget the fact that humans built the PC and programmed the software. Therefore, the 'dualism' so to speak, is offloaded onto 'us'. But in the brain this is not the case, and to argue that it is the case is merely to (covertly) posit a homunculus that gets everything working. Ultimately, therefore cognitivism, and, therefore, EP is Cartesian through and through. The fact that cognitivists and Evolutionary Psychologists declare that they are 'past' or 'over' Cartesianism is irrelevant. As Descombes puts it: 'declarations are not enough'.

The New Psychology

Whatever else one might say about it, 'New Psychology' or 4EA psychology, or enactivism, or whatever one wishes to call it, is, essentially, a way to get beyond Cartesian Dualism by 'undercutting' it (as neither cognitivism, nor behaviourism, nor psycho-analysis, was able to do).

Specifically, the 'New Psychologists' are attempting to get beyond the fundamental dualism of the 'inner and the outer', but as well as this, they are attempting to get beyond the other dualisms that afflicted cognitivism: of 'mind and body', 'person and environment', 'rationality and emotions' and the 'individual and society'. There is also a 'new' view of language associated with this new movement (discursive psychology) but that won't be discussed too much here.

So: what is the nature of this challenge? And is it true? To reiterate: the argument that I will be pursuing here is that if the anti-cognitivist 'new psychology' is a correct (or at least, less incorrect) description of cognition then cognitivism and therefore EP will have to go.

To begin at the beginning.

The Mind and the Body

Embodiment is, like Cognitivism, an attempt to get beyond Cartesian dualism, but, I will argue, unlike cognitivism, it is a successful attempt. Specifically, 'embodiment' is a way of getting beyond the Cartesian Dualism of *the Mind and the Body*.

Embodiment has its roots in Continental Psychology, but it is also similar to Brooks' 'new' AI, and the enactivist views of vision we saw proposed by Noë. However, in recent years, embodiment is most strongly associated with the work of the linguist George Lakoff and the philosopher Mark Johnson.

Lakoff and Johnson, in their classic work *Metaphors we Live By*, (Lakoff and Johnson, 1980) began by noting that we use metaphors all the time: a seemingly unremarkable observation. However, they went on to point out that almost all language is illiminably metaphorically even when the metaphors are, so to speak, hidden (for example 'I shot down his arguments', is metaphorical, but then so is 'Your claims are *indefensible.*' 'He *attacked* every weak point in my argument'. 'His criticisms were right on *target.*' '*I demolished* his argument', 'I've never *won* an argument with him' and so forth, all based on the fundamental metaphor of 'argument is war'). Lakoff and Johnson then went on to point out that many of these metaphorical constructs derive from bodily states or actions: war in the example above, but there are others: for example 'I'm feeling down 'implies that lying down (asleep or dead) is a bad thing to be, whereas 'I'm standing tall!' implies the opposite. They then went on to argue that since, in a very real sense, language is thought, cognition derives in a non-trivial way from our embodied states. Therefore unembodied cognition is a contradiction in terms.

This argument seems strange to us, or at least to most psychologists. For example, in the science fiction movie *2001: A Space Odyssey* nobody bursts out laughing when the digital computer HAL speaks and has conversations with the astronauts, despite the fact that HAL has no body. We take it for granted that, at least in theory, 'HAL' could in fact think, and this is a staple of science fiction, from Skynet in the Terminator movies to the Architect in the Matrix movies. And, of course, the whole theory of GOFAI (and thus cognitivism) presupposes that bodiless thought is possible. The theory of embodiment states that this is an impossibility: 'one' cannot think without a body because thinking is a form of 'being in the world': a form of *physically acting* in the world.

Again, there is no room here to go into the huge amount of empirical data that supports this thesis, although the interested reader should look up work by Andy Clark and Michael Wheeler (Clark, 2008; Wheeler, 2005) amongst many others. The key point is that not only does this explain more things that cognitivism, by seeing the difference between man and animal as being analogue rather than digital, this view genuinely crosses the Cartesian divide, and is, therefore, more Darwinian, I would argue, than 'classic' cognitivism. Note: after a notorious review of a political book of Lakoff's, Pinker and Lakoff did eventually 'lock swords' and debate this issue, but, given that the framework was political rather than philosophical, not much light was shed on the basic issues. However, Lakoff did write: 'The process of thinking is not algorithmic symbol manipulation, but rather neural computation, using brain mechanisms' (Lakoff, 2006), I agree with him, and I would also go on to argue that Pinker's solution to this problem (i.e. the brain is neural computation, but algorithmic symbol manipulation, as it were, 'floats on top of it') won't work, as argued in the last chapter.

The Somatic Marker Hypothesis

Our next Dualism has not spawned a new 'science' as such, but, instead, a new hypothesis, which is associated with the Portuguese/American psychologist Antonio Damasio. Nevertheless it challenges yet another Dualism that, yet again, has its roots in Descartes, but, yet again, has 'precursors' that go back to Plato.

Since Plato, the originator of Western Rationalism, it has long been assumed in the West that it is better to be *rational* than *irrational*. This presupposes a Dualistic idea: the antipathy of 'reason' and 'emotion'. And yet again, this follows from ideas we should by now be familiar with. To reiterate, the analogy between mathematical logic and 'cognition' led not just to a definition of truth, but to a definition of rationality.

Rationality, it seemed, was to behave as 'logically' as possible (and this use of logic was not to be taken metaphorically: it means, as much as possible 'in lines with the "rules" of Western logic, or maths, or both'). Rationality was, therefore, perceived as being a 'higher' thought process and was thus contrasted with 'emotion' (a 'lower' process). Emotions, it seemed, 'dragged us down': the road to Truth was to be as rational (logical) as possible.

Actually, as John McCrone has pointed out, 'irrationality' *per se* is something of a myth (McCrone, 1994). Which is merely a backwards, so to speak, way of pointing out that *rationality*, per se, is also a myth. The only way in which this belief in rationality could be justified was by demonstrating that 'higher' cognition consisted of algorithms manipulating symbols, in a way similar to, or identical to, mathematical logic: which is, of course the essence of cognitivism. But we have seen that this view makes no sense. Therefore, *pure* rationality, located inside the brain, simply does not occur, so to speak, 'in the wild'.[4]

Instead, as Damasio has pointed out, our so-called rational thinking always and invariably has an 'emotional' substrate. Damasio has studied patients with damage to the ventro-medial part of the pre-frontal cortex: i.e. The part of the brain associated with emotions. These patients, although being 'rational' in most respects (indeed, super-rational) nonetheless end up behaving in ways that *we* would consider to be profoundly *ir*rational (Damasio, 1994). Interestingly, in the 'somatic marker hypothesis', Damasio went on to argue that our decisions are made, in part, on the basis of our own self-observation of our somatic (i.e. embodied) states. Therefore, there is a profound link between 'rationality', 'affect' (emotions) and our embodied states: it is, therefore meaningless to consider these aspects of cognition separately, although of course one can and should look at the complex inter-relationships between them.

---

4 Which is simply another way of point out that mathematical logic exists, but it was *invented* by humans in order to perform specific tasks.

Damasio's ideas are fascinating, but, in the final analysis, like so many thinkers in the West, he still chooses to see human beings as predominantly atomised individuals, as opposed to truly social beings. This brings us to our next Dualism.

The Social

The third key Dualism of Cognitivism is that between Humans and Society. Due to their strange desire to model psychology on 18th century physics, cognitivists conceptualised human beings as 'atoms' engaging in simple causal relations with other atomised human beings. There was, therefore, a fundamental 'gap' between the human and society. 'Distributed Cognition' attempts to challenge this view, by seeing human beings as being *fundamentally* sociated (Hutchins, 1995).

Again this doesn't mean simply making the trivial observation that human beings have societies. It means that the atomistic, reductionistic way of looking at human beings, in which the individual is the key component (as always, the metaphor here is with Newtonian physics and Greek materialism, with humans here as being similar to atoms) is rejected. Instead, what is being argued here is that human beings are fundamentally and ineluctably social, and that to abstract a 'single' human being out of his/her society is in fact a profoundly unnatural way of looking at things.

For empirical evidence of this we should turn to the social psychology tradition generally, but also the work of Roger Barker.

Barker did much work in psychology, which has unfortunately not been as influential as it might have been. This is not because it is not theoretically interesting, or empirically grounded: it is both. But it *is* because it challenges one of the very basic assumptions of cognitivist orthodoxy, the idea that the individual should be the basic unit of analysis. But now people are looking at Barker's work again: I like to think he will become more influential as his radical theorising is understood.

Barker began by setting up a 'station' in the Kansas town of Oskaloosa, in which he and his fellow psychologists could study almost the entirety of the town as a social phenomenon. After much research they made a rather radical discovery: the behaviour of individuals in a given setting resembled the behaviour of other individuals in the same setting more than it did the *same* individual's in a *different* setting. Or as Barker put it: 'when people are in [a] "post office," they behave post office, and when they are in [a] "basketball game," they behave basketball game' [Scott, 2005: 321]).

It was this insight that led Barker to posit the idea of a behaviour setting, which he then went on to argue should be the basic unit of analysis for psychology (in other words, the equivalent for the cell for biology or the atom for physics... *replacing* the individual, which is normally taken as being the equivalent in psychology). Another key point is that Barker talks about 'standing patterns of behaviour' (i.e. the dynamic behaviours that people produce, seeing people as being dynamic, not static). A behaviour setting is the interface between the standing pattern of behaviour, and the milieu (i.e. environment), where the milieu matches the standing pattern of behaviour and vice versa. For example, look at a doctor's waiting room. Without patients or the possibility of patients, it is no longer a waiting room. It's just a room. But likewise, the kinds of behaviour that are appropriate and therefore engaged in by the people in it, are facilitated and enabled by the room. The two are linked, dialectically so to speak. You can't talk about the people without the environment but equally you can't discuss the environment without the people in it (Barker, 1966).

The implications of this are that people are radically social, rather than just being social by chance, or to facilitate individualistic desires. To bring the subject back to AI, this is another reason why HAL from 2001 could never exist. Not only does HAL not have a body, but HAL has no society (that is, no society of other computers).

Further evidence for this view comes from the Activity Theory tradition descending from Vygotsky. Vygotsky was one of the key intellectual opponents of Piaget, who we have already looked at. Now: Piaget provided many profound insights into development, and his evolutionary approach (in the broadest sense of the word: that is, seeing evolution not just in the macro-level, but on the micro-level as well, i.e. in terms of our own development) is a profound insight and vital in terms of a genuinely scientific psychology.

But Vygotsky argued, (and provided much experimental evidence to back this view up) that Piaget's emphasis on egocentric speech was misguided (Vygotsky, 1978). Piaget emphasised that the child began with egocentric, 'internal' speech, and that social speech developed out of this. Vygotsky argued the contrary, that speech is fundamentally and ineluctably a social phenomenon, and that our own 'inner monologue' is an adaption of pre-existing external social dialogue. In other words, outer speech with others comes first: our inner musings come after. Speech is social, and our 'inner monologue' is an adaption of external speech. But because thought is, to a very large extent, based on language, this would prove that thought is also, therefore, ineluctably social. Vygotsky also argued that Piaget saw the 'evolution' of the child in an overly deterministic fashion: instead environmental factors and triggers could 'speed up' 'slow down' or otherwise affect child cognitive development. Vygotsky founded an important and growing school of psychology, Activity Theory, that to the best of my knowledge none of the major thinkers of EP have ever alluded to. This is a pity, as their writings challenge EP at its core (Vygotsky, 1978).

Therefore what is being argued here is that human beings are not digital computers. Instead they are biological entities who are (and this is therefore true by definition) embodied, and social, like all other animals.

Finally, we have the Dualism between human beings and the Environment, which again follows from the Newtonian/ Cartesian assumptions. To quote Bracken and Thomas:

Descartes distinguished between the *res cogitans* and the *res extensa*. The former referred to the soul or mind and was said to be essentially 'a thing which thinks.' The latter was the material stuff of the body. It was characterised primarily by the fact of extension: it occupied space and was therefore amenable to measurement. In recent years neuroscientists and cognitive psychologists have argued that this ontological separation of mind and body is no longer tenable. The former maintain that mental functions can be fully explained by brain science. The latter make the case for a distinct psychological realm but one whose operations, like those of computer software, are measurable and open to scientific investigation. The *res cogitans* is illusive no longer. We can map it, scan it, and explain its functions in biological or computational terms.

These ideas have become dominant in medical circles and, in some form or other, have become articles of faith for most doctors, psychiatrists, and psychologists. Contemporary philosophers such as Paul and Patricia Churchland and Jerry Fodor offer support for this position. Many philosophers disagree, however, and point out that, although it claims to get us beyond ontological dualism, this doctrine really keeps alive the essential features of Descartes' philosophy. In particular, it continues his epistemological separation of inner mind from outside world. It also fails to recognise the problems involved in regarding the mind as a 'thing' – Descartes' *res*. (Bracken and Thomas, 2002).

Situated Cognition

It is this view that has been challenged by the new science of Situated Cognition (Clancey, 1997). To quote from the article that commenced this new approach:

Many teaching practices implicitly assume that conceptual knowledge can be abstracted from the situations in which it is learned and used. This article argues that this assumption inevitably limits the effectiveness of such practices. Drawing on recent research into cognition as it is manifest in everyday activity, the authors argue that knowledge is situated, being in

> part a product of the activity, context, and culture in which it
> is developed and used' (Brown *et al.*, 1989).

For teaching practices, needless to say, one might also substitute 'psychologists'. And the phrase 'conceptual' (i.e. abstract, 'rational') knowledge, demonstrates the Cartesian roots of this idea. As we saw earlier, it was one of the 'attractions' of cognitivism that, in propounding a vision of epistemology, it also gave one, free, so to speak, a vision of ontology, and, more specifically, a definition of 'Truth'. And it was a key attraction of this Truth that this version of Truth was not to be contextualisable. Things were 'true' or not if the inner 'mental model' 'mapped' onto reality, and this was true regardless of the 'context' of the mental model (or the fragment of reality being 'mapped onto'). Truth, therefore became (to use the jargon) non 'observer specific'.

Situated cognition argues against this view. As one might imagine, given its philosophical underpinnings, situated cognition tends to use methods closer to sociology than experimental psychology per se, and therefore a single, 'killer' experiment to prove its value is lacking. Nonetheless, the studies carried out by psychologists in this tradition are fascinating, and, if read with an open mind, persuasive. For example, Lave and Wenger's studies of various 'communities of practice' (for example tailors, midwives and ex-alcoholics) provides evidence for learning being a social and situated practice that occurs *in the world*, as opposed to being a solitary, conceptual, individual 'abstract' 'logical' phenomenon (Lave, 1988: Wenger *et al.*, 2002).

Where do we go from here?

So: where we should go from here?

There are three basic points that must be made here. All of them are controversial, and yet they must be asked, or else psychology will never make the progress it craves: for the worst of all possible worlds would be for psychology to ditch cognitivism and 'EP' only to replace them with something else that is in its own way just as flawed.

The first question that must be asked is: does psychology actually *need* an overarching, 'meta-theory'? Again, we must not be misled by metaphor here. The idea that it does is based on the idea that elaborate meta-theories (and of course here we think automatically of Newtonian physics or relativity) guide theoretical physics, and that, because psychology 'must' aspire to the precision of physics (or chemistry, at a push) then a similar kind of mathematical theory 'must' be created to 'guide' psychology, or at least to have as an over-arching framework for research.

One might add here that Pinker *et al.* ignore the work of (for example) Nancy Cartwright (1999). Cartwright has challenged the view of science in which science is viewed as a pyramid with 'theoretical physics' at the top, which, of course, all the other sciences must aspire to. Instead, she paints a picture of the sciences as being more like a patchwork quilt, with no 'one' science being in a pre-eminent situation, and with methodologies tied into to task requirements, not being 'pre-judged' and then used regardless, the 'one size fits all' model of science. What Cartwright (and others, such as Kuhn) have shown is that scientific progress is far from being the linear, rational process presupposed by cognitivism and EP, and that sociological and psychological influences are also important. The success of theoretical physics has been due to sociological and political factors as well as its use of mathematics, as well as certain advantages available *due to its subject matter.*

One might also add that, yet again, the view of science held by EP is absurdly 18th century. At the moment, for example, physics HAS no 'guiding' meta-theory. It has two theories, quantum physics and relativity, which are incompatible with each other, and moreover, philosophically contradictory. There is no reason apart from blind faith to think that they will ever be reconciled (this is not to say they won't be, nor that the attempt to unite them should stop, merely to point out that the idea that they *will* be reconciled at some point in the future is merely a pious wish). And yet physics continues to make progress and to be a worthwhile activity: which makes the point that perhaps sciences do not necessarily need meta-theories.

Another issue is the issue of laws. Cognitivism and EP presuppose that the laws of nature exist, that they are real (in some unspecified, perhaps Platonic way) and causal and that therefore, a law bound way is the only 'true' way to understand human behaviour: this led them to think that the idea of 'laws' or 'rules' existing in the human brain, having a causal relationship with behaviour was the only way for a truly 'scientific' psychology to exist and that (the fateful link!) these rules were similar or identical to the algorithms used by digital computers.

But many modern philosophers of science question the existence of these 'laws of physics' or even 'laws of nature'. After all, like causality (another 'thing' whose existence has been questioned since Hume) we never actually 'observe' these laws in any shape or form. Instead they are inferred ex post facto. But if we only observe their effects, how can we grant them causal powers? Surely only material objects have them? Moreover, unless we genuinely grant the Laws of Nature Platonic status (i.e. they predate the existence of the Cosmos) then we are again in a situation of infinite regress: what 'caused' these laws? More laws...and so forth. Philosophers such as Bas van Fraassen suggest that, rather than the foundation stone of modern science, the concept of the laws of nature are in fact merely a hangover from Platonic metaphysics, in the same way that our obsession with introducing mathematics into science, perhaps, ultimately, stems from Pythagorean number mysticism. (van Fraassen, 1980).

Towards an Evolutionary Psychology

Finally one last point must be made: even though psychology perhaps does not need an overarching theory and, may never have one, it can't do any harm for psychologists to go back to Darwin, to look at what a genuine evolutionary psychology might look like. Psychology will not be and should not be reducible to biology. Nevertheless an evolutionary viewpoint might well be another worthwhile weapon in the psychologist's armoury. But this would have to be a *genuinely* evolutionary psychology, based on biology, as opposed to EP's attempts to create a psychology based on computer science and then graft some Darwinian rhetoric onto it. And what better approach here than actually going back to Darwin? But we should look at not the better known of Darwin's works but as Alan Costall argues, his fascinating work on worms.

In a seminal essay entitled 'From Darwin to Watson (and Cognitivism) and back again: the principle of animal-environment mutuality.' Costall (2004) points out some things that have been pointed out over and over again in this essay: for example, the continuities between behaviourism and cognitivism, the fact that 'Cognitive psychology has also remained committed to a very old-fashioned notion of scientific method' and so on.

But he continues:

> Darwin's remarkable achievement was to reconcile the concepts of transformation and … design. He explained adaptation in terms of transformation (and, conversely, transformation in terms of adaptation) and, for good measure, he managed to explain unity of type in terms of commonality of descent. Yet this was not just a question of the one-sided assimilation of design into the pre-existing schema of mechanistic science. When Darwin introduced the concept of adaptation into the discourse of natural science, he also undermined the dualism of subject and object at the heart of both Cartesian mechanistic science and Cartesian mentalist psychology.

> So much has happened since Darwin (not least the hijacking of Darwinism by traditional mechanistic science) that it easy to forget the profound impact his work initially had upon psychology precisely because Darwin had not been trained as a psychologist. As his protégé, George Romanes, suggested:

'Mr. Darwin was not only not himself a psychologist, but had little aptitude for, and perhaps less sympathy with, the technique of psychological method. The whole constitution of his mind was opposed to the subtlety of the distinctions and the mysticism of the conceptions which this technique so frequently involves; and therefore he was accustomed to regard the problems of mind in the same broad and general light that *he regarded all the other problems of nature*. (Romanes, 1882, pp. 65–66 emphasis added)'.

In addition to Darwin's treatment of mind as inherent to the natural order of things (Allen, 1983; Richards, 1987; Schweber, 1985; Smith, 1978), there was his specific emphasis upon the fact of adaptation: the co-ordination of organism and environment. Here is John Dewey discussing the impact of biological thinking on the 'new psychology' as early as 1884, just two years after Darwin's death: 'We see that man is somewhat more than a neatly dovetailed psychical machine who may be taken as an isolated individual, laid on the dissecting table of analysis and duly anatomized. To biology is due the conception of organism. In psychology this conception has led to the recognition of mental life as an organic unitary process developing according to the laws of all life, and not a theatre for the exhibition of independent faculties, or a rendezvous in which isolated sensations and ideas may gather, hold external converse, and then forever part. Along with this recognition of the solidarity of mental life has come that of the relation in which it stands to other lives organized in society'.

Costall points out that in Darwin's experiments with earthworms

invite us to think differently about the relation between animal and environment, for even within so-called ecological approaches to psychology it is easy to slip into a kind of environmental determinism and reify the environment as an 'independent variable' external to the animal in question. Animal and environment are interdependent, however, and this is not just a question of logic or definition but of history, 'a moving, growing never finished process' (Dewey, 1958,

p. 295). Earthworms, through their collective activity, have both transformed and sustained their circumstances. Earthworms and the vegetable mould surrounding them have co-evolved. Vegetable mould simply did not exist before the evolution of earthworms. Their relation is mutual. 'In his (work) Earthworms [Darwin's] attention was drawn to that aspect of ecology which at that time and still many years later was neglected by ecologists. Ecology, according to its very definition, studies interaction and interrelationships of organisms and their environments. Up to a short time ago, ecologists only studied dependence of organisms on their environment. Darwin in his Earthworms has shown brilliantly the other side of the medal – the influence of organisms on their environment, i.e. the dependence of the milieu, of the environment, on their activity.' (Ghilarov, 1983, pp. 3–4) (Costall, 2004).

The truth is, that as the above indicates, Darwinian biology, and, hence, genuine Darwinian psychology, is anti-Cartesian and anti-homuncular to its core. It is far more compatible with the view of human cognition posited by situated cognition and the other views discussed above than it is with Cognitivism. This suggests that, whereas Darwin casts a long, and increasing, shadow over 21st century psychology, it will only be possible to genuinely assimilate his ideas when the cognitivist orthodoxy is finally overthrown, and a genuinely scientific approach to cognition is developed. When this is done, and a genuine Evolutionary Psychology arises, 'EP' will be relegated to a footnote in psychological history, where it belongs.

Bibliography

Aizawa, K. (1997) Explaining Systematicity, *Mind and Language*, 12, 115–136

Allen, G. E. (1983). The several faces of Darwin: Materialism in nineteenth and twentieth century evolutionary theory. In D. S. Bendall (Ed)., *Evolution from Molecules to Men* (pp. 81–102), Cambridge: Cambridge University Press.

American Heritage Dictionary (accessed 2009) Definition of Algorithm. Online: http://dictionary.reference.com/browse/algorithm

Barker, R. (1966). *One Boy's Day*. New York: Shoe String Press.

Barkow, J., Cosmides, L. and Tooby, J. (1992). *The Adapted Mind: Evolutionary psychology and the generation of culture.* NY: Oxford University Press.

Barres B. (2008). The Mystery and Magic of Glia: A Perspective on Their Roles in Health and Disease, *Neuron*, 60, November 6, 2008 Available online http://download.cell.com/images/edimages/neuron/pdf/barres.PDF

Barret, H. and Kurzban, R. (2006) Modularity in Cognition. *Psychological Review*, 113, 3, 629–647.

Block, N. (1980) Troubles with Functionalism, in, *Readings in Philosophy of Psychology*. Cambridge, MA: Harvard University Press.

Boden, M. (2006) *Mind as Machine, Volume 1.* Oxford, OUP.

Bracken P. and Philip Thomas J (2002) Time to Move Beyond the Mind-body Split, *BMJ*, 325, 1433–1434

Brooks, R. (1990) Elephants Don't Play Chess, *Robotics and Autonomous Systems*, 6, 3–15

Broughton, J., and Carriero, J. (2007). *A Companion to Descartes.* London: John Wiley and Sons.

Brown, J. S. Collins, A. and Duguid, S. (1989) Situated Cognition and the Culture of Learning, *Educational Researcher* 18, 1, 32–42.

Buller, D. (2005) *Adapting Minds: Evolutionary Psychology and the Persistent Quest for Human Nature.* Cambridge, MA: MIT Press.

Burtt, E.A. (1967). *The Metaphysical Foundations of Modern Physical Science: A historical and critical essay.* London: Routledge & Kegan Paul. (First edition 1924)

Buss, D.M. (1994) *The Evolution of Desire: Strategies of Human Mating.* New York: Basic Books.

Cartwright, N. (1999). *The Dappled World.* Cambridge: CUP.

Chalmers, D. (1991) Why Fodor and Pylyshyn Were Wrong: The Simplest Refutation. *Proceedings of the Twelfth Annual Conference of the Cognitive Science Society*, pp. 340–347.

Chomsky, Noam (1957) Syntactic Structures, The Hague/Paris: Mouton. pp. 15.

Chomsky, N. (1966), *Cartesian Linguistics*, New York: Harper and Row.

Chomsky, N. (1967) 'A Review of B. F. Skinner's *Verbal Behavior*' In Leon A. Jakobovits and Murray S. Miron (eds.), *Readings in the Psychology of Language*, New Jersey: Prentice-Hall, , pp. 142–143

Chomsky, N. (1980) *Rules and Representations*, Columbia, Columbia University Press.

Clancey, W. (1997) *Situated cognition: on human knowledge and computer representations*, Cambridge: Cambridge University Press,

Clark, A. (2008) *Supersizing the Mind.* Oxford: Oxford University Press.

Cosmides, L and Tooby J. (1987) From Evolution to Behaviour: Evolutionary Psychology as the Missing Link. In Dupre (ed) *The Latest on the Best: Essays on Evolution and Optimality.* London: MIT Press.

Costall, A. (2004). From Darwin to Watson (and Cognitivism) and back again: the principle of animal-environment mutuality. *Behavior & Philosophy*, 32, 179–195

Costall, A. (2007). How Will we Know When we Have Become Post-Cognitivists? In *The Mind, the Body and the World,* (Eds Anderson, T., Davies, J. Ross, A., and Wallace B.) pp. 163–179. London: Imprint Academic.

Crevier, D. (1993), *AI: The Tumultuous Search for Artificial Intelligence*, New York, NY: BasicBook

Crowder, R. (1982) The Demise of Short-term Memory, *Acta Psychologica*, 50, 291.

Cziko, G. (2000). *The Things We Do*. Massachusetts: MIT Press.

Damasio, A. (1994) *Descartes' Error: Emotion, Reason, and the Human Brain*, Putnam Publishing, 1994

Darwin, C. (1881) *The Formation of Vegetable Mould, Through the Action of Worms with Observations on their Habits*. London: John Murray.

David, A. (2000) *The Experience of Ancient Egypt*, London: Routledge

Dewey J.(1896) The Reflex Arc Concept in Psychology, *Psychological Review*, 3, 357–370

Davis, J. and Hersh, R. (1987) *Descartes' Dream*. New York: Mariner Books.

Deacon, T. (1997) *The Symbolic Species*. London, Penguin.

Dennett, D. (1999) Dennett's Deal, in *Edge Magazine*, 56. Available online: http://www.edge.org/documents/archive/edge56.html

Descombes, V. (2001). *The Mind's Provisions*. Princeton: Princeton University Press.

Dewey, J. (1958). *Experience and Nature*. New York: Dover. (Based on the Paul Carus lectures of 1925)

Fodor, J. and Pylyshyn, Z. (1983). *Modularity of Mind: An Essay on Faculty Psychology*. Cambridge, Mass.: MIT Press

Dalhousie University (2002) *Jerome H. Barkow Webpage.* retrieved 18th August 2009, URL http://sociologyandsocialanthropology. dal.ca/Faculty/Jerome_Barkow.php

Devlin, K. (2003) *The Language of Mathematics*. London: Macmillan.

Dobbs, D. (2005). Fact or Phrenology? *Scientific American Mind*, 16, 1, 24–31. Available online: http://www.scientificamerican.com/ article.cfm?id=fact-or-phrenology

Dodge, N. (2007) *The Brian that Changes Itself*. London, Penguin.

Dreyfus, H. (1992) *What Computers Still Can't Do*. Cambridge, MA, MIT Press.

Everett, D. (2005) Cultural Constraints on Grammar and Cognition in Pirahã: Another Look at the Design Features of Human Language, *Current Anthropology* 46: 621–646

Falcon, A. (2008). Aristotle on Causality. *Stanford Encyclopedia of Philosophy.* http://plato.stanford.edu/entries/aristotle-causality/

Faye, J. (2008). Copenhagen Interpretation of Quantum Physics, in the *Stanford Encyclopedia of Philosophy*. Online: http://plato. stanford.edu/entries/qm-copenhagen/

Fodor, J. (1974) Special Sciences, *Synthese* 28, 97–11

Fodor, J. (1983) *The Modularity of Mind*. Massachussetts: MIT Press.

Fodor, J. (2000) *The Mind Doesn't Work That Way: The Scope and Limits of Computational Psychology,* Cambridge, MA, MIT Press.

Fodor, J. and Pylyshyn, Z. (1981). How Direct is Visual Perception? Some Reflections on Gibson's 'Ecological Approach'. *Cognition, 9,* 139–96.

Francis, R. (2004) *Why Men Won't Ask for Directions: the seductions of sociobiology.* Princeton: Princeton University Press.

Friesen, N. and Feenberg, A. (2007) "Ed Tech in Reverse": Information Technologies and the Cognitive Revolution. *Educational Philosophy and Theory,* 39, 7, 720–736.

Galilei, G. (2007). Letter to the Grand Duchess Christina, and the Assayer. In Martinich, A. Allhoff, F., and Vaidya, J. (Eds), *Early modern philosophy: essential readings with commentary.* London: Wiley-Blackwood.

Gentner, T. Q., Fenn, K. M., Margoliash, D., and Nusbaum, H. C. (2006) Recursive syntactic pattern learning by songbirds. *Nature,* 440:1204–1207.

Ghilarov, M. S. (1983). Darwin's Formation of Vegetable Mould- its philosophical basis. In J. E. Satchell (Ed.), *Earthworm ecology: From Darwin to vermiculture* (pp. 1–4). London: Chapman & Hall.

Glenberg, Arthur M. (1997) What memory is for, *Behavioural and Brain Sciences,* 20, 1–55

Goldman A. (Ed) (1993) *Readings in Philosophy and Cognitive Science.* Massachusetts: MIT Press.

Gould, E., Alison, J., Reeves, J., Michael, S., Graziano, A., Gross, C. (1999) Neurogenesis in the Neocortex of Adult Primates, *Science,* 286, 5439, pp. 548–552.

Greenberg, J. (2000) *Indo-European and its closest relatives: the Eurasiatic language family, vol. 1: grammar.* Stanford: Stanford University Press

Harvard University (2003) *Steven Pinker, Long Bio.* retrieved 18th August 2009, URL http://pinker.wjh.harvard.edu/about/longbio.html

Hawking, S. and Penrose, R (2000) *The Nature of Space and Time,* Princeton: Princeton University Press.

Hebb, Donald (1960), 'The American revolution', *American Psychologist,* 15, pp. 735–745

Heft, H. (2001). *Ecological psychology in context: James Gibson, Roger Barker, and the legacy of William James's radical empiricism.* Philadelphia: Lawrence Erlbaum.

Hobson, J. (2004). *The Eastern Origins of Western Civilisation.*

Cambridge: CUP.

Hutchins, E. (1995) *Cognition in the Wild*, Massachussetts: MIT Press.

Ketelaar, T. and Todd, P.M. (2001) Framing our thoughts: Ecological rationality as evolutionary psychology's answer to the frame problem. In Holcomb III, H.R. (Eds.) *Conceptual Challenges in Evolutionary Psychology: Innovative Research Strategies*, pp. 179–211. Kluwer Publishers.

King, D. (1997) *Kasparov Vs Deeper Blue*. London: Batsford.

Klein, G., and Calderwood, R. (1988), 'How do people use analogies?' In Kolodner J. (Ed.) *Case-based Reasoning: Proceedings of a Workshop on Case-Based Reasoning*, May 10–13 Clearwater Beach Florida. San Mateo: Morgan Kaufman Publishers.

Kotchoubey, B. (2000) About hens and eggs. Perception and action, psychology and neuroscience: a reply to Michaels, *Ecological Psychology*, 13, 22, 135–141.

Kotchoubey, B., (2005) Event-related potentials, cognition, and behavior: A biological approach, *Brain and Behavioral Sciences*, 42–65

Koyre, A. (1965). *Newtonian Studies*. London: Chapman & Hall.

Krüger, L., Daston, L., Heidelberger, M., Gigerenzer, G., and Morgan, M. (1987) *The Probabilistic Revolution, Vols 1 and 2*, Massachussetts, MIT Press.

Kukla A. and Walmsley, J (2006) *Mind: a historical and philosophical introduction to the major theories*, Indianapolis, Hackett Publishing.

Lachman, J, and Butterfield, E., (1979), *Cognitive Psychology and Information Processing*. Philadelphia, Lawrence Erlbaum.

Lakoff, G. (2006) *A Response to Steven Pinker*. Available online: http://www.powells.com/biblio?show=HARDCOVER:NEW:0374158282:23.00&page=authorsnote

Lakoff, G. and Johnson, M. (1980). *Metaphors We Live By*. Chicago: University of Chicago Press.

Lave, Jean (1988). *Cognition in practice: mind, mathematics and culture in everyday life*. New York: Cambridge University Press

Levin, J. (2009). Functionalism. In *The Stanford Encyclopedia of Philosophy*. http://plato.stanford.edu/entries/functionalism/

Lighthill, J. (2001). Artificial Intelligence: a General Survey. In Chrisley R. (Ed). *Artificial Intelligence: Critical Concepts*. London: Taylor and Francis.

Malik, K (2001). *Man Beast and Zombie*. London: Phoenix.

Markoff, John (14 October 2005), Behind Artificial Intelligence, a

Squadron of Bright, Real People, *The New York Times*, retrieved 16 October 2008

Marr, A. (1982) *Vision*. London: Freeman and Co.

McCarthy J., Minsky, M. L., Rochester N. Shannon C.E. (1955). *A Proposal for the Dartmouth Summer Research Project on Artificial Intelligence* Available online http://www-formal.stanford.edu/jmc/history/dartmouth/dartmouth.html

McCarthy, J. (1996). *The Qualification Problem*. In Circumscription: A Form of Non-Monotonic Reasoning. Stanford University. Available online: ttp://www-formal.stanford.edu/jmc/circumscription/node1.html#SECTION00010000000000000000

McCarthy J. and Hayes, P. (1969) *Some Philosophical Problems from the Standpoint of Artificial Intelligence*. Stanford University, Available online: http://www-formal.stanford.edu/jmc/mcchay69.pdf

McClelland, J.L., Rumelhart, D.E. and the PDP research group (1986) *Parallel distributed processing: Explorations in the microstructure of cognition. Volume II*. Cambridge, MA: MIT Press.

McClelland J. and Seidenberg, M. (2000) Why do Kids say Goed and Brang?, *Science,* Volume 287, Number 5450, January 7th issue, pp. 47–48.

McCrone, J (1994) *The Myth of Irrationality*. London: Carrol and Graf.

Maslin, K. (2001). *An Introduction to the Philosophy of Mind*. London: Wiley-Blackwell.

Minsky, M. (1967). *Computation: Finite and Infinite Machines,* NJ: Prentice-Hall.

Minsky, M. and Papert, M. (1969). *Perceptrons; an introduction to computational geometry*. Massachussetts. MIT Press.

Modgil, C. (1967). *B.F. Skinner: Consensus and Controversy*. London: Routledge.

Moore, T. and Carling, C. (1982) *Understanding Language*. London: Macmillan.

Neisser, U. (1967) *Cognitive psychology*. New York: Appleton-Century-Crofts.

Nevins, A., Pesetsky, D., Rodrigues, C. (2009) Pirahã Exceptionality: A Reassessment . *Language*, 85, 2, 355–404

Newell, A., and Simon, H. (1972) *Human Problem Solving*. Englewood Cliffs, NJ: Prentice Hall.

Nisbett, R., and Wilson, T. (1977). Telling More than we Can Know. *Psychological Review,* 84, 3, 231–259.

Noë, A. (2005) *Action in Perception*. Massachussetts: MIT press.

Penrose, R. (1990) *The Emperor's New Mind*. Oxford: OUP.

Papadakis, N. and Plexousakis, D. (2002) Actions with Duration and Constraints: The Ramification Problem in Temporal Databases. In *14th IEEE International Conference on Tools with Artificial Intelligence* (ICTAI'02).

Pinker, S. (1994) *The Language Instinct: How the Mind Creates Language*. New York: WilliamMorrow.

Pinker, S. (2003) *How the Mind Works*. London: Penguin.

Putnam, H. (1975) The 'Innateness Hypothesis' and Explanatory Models in Linguistics. In Stich, S. (Ed) *Innate Ideas*, 133–144. Berkeley: University of California Press.

Richards, R. J. (1987). *Darwin and the Emergence of Evolutionary Theories of Mind and Behavior*. Chicago, IL: University of Chicago Press.

Riesbeck, C., and Schank. R. (1989) *Inside Case-based Reasoning*. Northvale, NJ: Erlbaum, 1989.

Romanes, G. J. (1882). Work in psychology. In T. H. Huxley, G. J. Romanes, A. Geikie, & W. T. Thiselton Dyer (Eds.), *Charles Darwin: Memorial notices reprinted from Nature*, pp. 65–80, London: Macmillan.

Rosch, E., (1978) Principles of Categorization, in Rosch, E. & Lloyd, B.B. (eds), *Cognition and Categorization*, pp. 27–48, Hillsdale: Lawrence Erlbaum Associates.

Rumelhart, D.E., McClelland, J.L. and the PDP research group (1986) *Parallel distributed processing: Explorations in the microstructure of cognition. Volume I*. Cambridge, MA: MIT Press.

Schweber, S. S. (1985). The Wider British Context in Darwin's Theorizing. In D. Kohn (Ed.), *The Darwinian heritage*, pp. 35–69, Princeton: Princeton University Press.

Scott, M. (2005) A Powerful Theory and a Paradox: ecological psychologists after Barker', *Environment and Behavior*, 37, 295–329.

Searle, John (1980) Minds, Brains and Programs, *Behavioral and Brain Sciences* 3, 3, 417–457.

Searle, J. (1990) Is the Brain a Digital Computer? *Proceedings and Addresses of the American Philosophical Association* 64: 21–37.

Shallice, T. and Warrington, E. (1970) Independent Functioning of Verbal Memory Stores: a neurophysiological study, *Quarterly Journal of Experimental Psychology*, 22, 261, 203.

Shermer, M. (2008) The Brian Is Not Modular, *Scientific American*, May. Available Online, URL: http://www.scientificamerican.com/article.cfm?id=a-new-phrenology

Shannon, C.E. (1948, July and October) A mathematical theory of communication, *Bell System Technical Journal*, vol. 27, pp. 379–423 and 623–656.

Simon, Herbert A. (1965). *The Shape of Automation for Men and Management*. New York: Harper and Row.

Simons, D. and Chabris, C. (1999) Gorillas in our Midst: Sustained inattentional blindness for dynamic events." *Perception*, 28, 1059–1074.

Skinner, B. (1991). *Verbal Behaviour*. Action: MA: Copley Publishing.

Smith, C. U. M. (1978) Charles Darwin, the origin of consciousness, and panpsychism. *Journal of the History of Biology*, 11, 245–267.

Solan, Z., Horn, D., Ruppin, E., and Edelman, S. (2005). Unsupervised learning of natural languages. *Proceedings of the National Academy of Sciences* 102 (33), 11629–11634.

Spelke, E. S., Hirst, W., and Neisser, U. (1976). Skills of divided attention. *Cognition, 4*, 215–230.

Sun, R. (1998). Artificial Intelligence. In Bechtel, W. & Graham, B. (eds.) *A Companion to Cognitive Science*. Malden, MA: Blackwell Publishers Ltd.

Tallis, R. (2004) *Why the Mind is not a Computer*. Exeter: Imprint Academic

Tooby, J. and Cosmides,L (1990). The Past Explains the Present. *Ethology and Sociobiology*, 11, 375–424.

Turing, A. M. (1937). On computable numbers, with an application to the Entscheidungsproblem. *Proceedings of the London Mathematical Society* Series 2, 42, 230–265

Turing, A.M. (1950). Computing machinery and intelligence. *Mind*, 59, 433–460.

UC Santa Barbara (2002) *Leda Cosmides' Webpage*, retrieved 18th August 2009, URL http://www.psych.ucsb.edu/people/faculty/cosmides/index.php

UC Santa Barbara (2004). *John Tooby's Webpage*, retrieved 18th August 2009, URL http://www.anth.ucsb.edu/faculty/tooby/

University of Texas at Austin (2009) *David Buss's Webpage*, retrieved 18th August 2009, http://homepage.psy.utexas.edu/homepage/Group/BussLAB/david_home.htm

Uttal, W. (2000) *The War Between Mentalism and Behaviourism*. Philadelphia, Lawrence Erlbaum.

van Fraassen, B. (1980) *The Scientific Image*, Oxford: Oxford University Press.

Varela, F., Thompson, E. and Rosch, E. (1991). *The Embodied Mind:*

Cognitive science and human experience. Cambridge MA: MIT Press.

Vygotsky, L. (1978) *Mind in Society.* Harvard: Harvard University Press.

Walker, M. (1999) Chiseling Competence: A connectionist revision of Chomsky's Language Acquisition Device. Thesis for Emory University.

Wallace, B. (2004) *Addiction.* Addiction Research and Theory, 12, 3, 195–199.

Wallace, B. and Ross, A. (2006) *Beyond Human Error.* Florida: CRC Press.

Wallace, B., Ross, A., Davies, J. and Anderson, T. (2007). *The Mind, the Body and the World.* London: Imprint Academic.

Watson, J. (1997) *Behaviourism.* New Brunswick: Transaction Publishers.

Wenger, E., McDermott, R. and Snyder, W. (2002) *Cultivating communities of practice: a guide to managing knowledge.* Cambridge, Mass.: Harvard Business School Press.

Wheeler, M. (2005) *Reconstructing the Cognitive World.* Massachussetts: MIT Press.

Wilson, M. D. (1980). Body and mind from the Cartesian point of view. In R. W. Rieber (Ed.), *Body and mind: Past, present, and future,* pp. 35–55, New York: Academic Press.

Whitehead, A. N. (1926). *Science and the Modern World:* Lowell Lectures, 1925. Cambridge: Cambridge University Press.

Wilson, E. (2000). *Sociobiology: The New Synthesis, 25th Anniversary Edition,* Cambridge Massachusetts, Harvard University Press.

Wilson, E. (2006). *Naturalist,* Washington DC: Island Press.

Young, R. M. (1966). Scholarship and the history of the behavioral sciences. *History of Science,* 5, 1–51.

Index